P9-DBR-255

THINK AGAIN

A Response to Fundamentalism's Claim on Christianity

For Leigh, who sees so clearly and loves so deeply;
for Cara, Lisa and Corinne, who remind me daily that
love is the most important part of life;
and for the people of University Congregational
Church, who give me the honor of walking by their
side on this amazing and beautiful faith journey.

THINK AGAIN

A Response to Fundamentalism's Claim on Christianity

DR. GARY COX

Published by University Congregational Press
9209 E. 29th St. N.
Wichita, KS 67226

Printed in the United States of America

ISBN: 0-9776268-0-6

Contents

About the Author

Soren Kiekegaard is famous for having said that religious conversions cannot be reduced to a single, mundane moment. But if one can learn of God while waiting for a traffic light to change or while shaving — perhaps he was wrong.

Gary Cox was a successful salesman living in Moore, Oklahoma, more than a decade ago when he decided to listen to a radio preacher in his bathroom while shaving. What he heard was one of my sermons, and a surprising message in the heart of the Bible Belt: *God's love is empowering and unconditional, whether we like it or not!*

Lucky for us, Gary put the razor down and called his wife Leigh to come and listen also. The two of them stood together in that bathroom and not only listened to the rest of the sermon, but journeyed to Mayflower Church in Oklahoma City to meet the messenger and the congregation.

So began a wonderful friendship, and the beginning of a call to ministry which changed his life, and the lives of countless others as well. Now in the pages of this book, you will meet the man whose clear vision and courageous voice have become an important component in the recovery and renewal of the church in our time.

When Gary Cox announced to me that he was going to attend Phillips Graduate Seminary, I was delighted for the future of the church — especially for thoughtful Protestantism, which is in danger. When he graduated with honors, I was not surprised, and when my father persuaded him to be a candidate for the pulpit of the church he had founded — University Congregational Church in Wichita, Kansas — I knew that a great and thoughtful congregation would be wonderfully served.

Now that Gary has completed his Doctor of Ministry Degree at the University of Chicago and preached a compelling series of sermons on the dangers of fundamentalism, it is fitting that they should be preserved in this book for readers both inside and outside the walls of the church.

Gary Cox's approach is radically inclusive insisting that no single stream of thought can lay exclusive claim to the Christian faith. He thinks and writes with a pastor's heart, and makes theology accessible as an act of love. What a privilege it is for me, as a mentor and friend, to write the first words of this book on his behalf.

His words will speak for themselves — and not a moment too soon.

Dr. Robin R. Meyers
Minister, Mayflower Congregational UCC Church, Oklahoma City
Professor of Rhetoric, Oklahoma City University
December 21, 2005

Acknowledgements

I am indebted to many people for the publication of this book. Dr. James Rhatigan was the first to encourage me to transform my 10-part sermon series on fundamentalism into a book. He then spearheaded the process, from concept through publication.

The people of University Congregational Church stood behind the project, offering encouragement and assistance every step of the way. I do not have the words to express what a blessing this congregation is in my life.

My wife, Leigh Cox, is not only the inspiration of my life, she also made the first edit on this book as it evolved from oral to written form. Connie White worked with my wife and me on the final edit and prepared the manuscript for publication.

And then there are those who have shaped my theological outlook. The great professors at both Phillips Theological Seminary and Chicago Theological Seminary have nurtured my faith, and the authors listed in the annotated bibliography have had a major impact on my faith journey. Two colleagues have left a deep impression on me, setting the bar high for the content of sermons: Dr. Robert Meyers, minister emeritus at University Congregational Church, and Dr. Robin Meyers, senior minister of Mayflower Congregational Church in Oklahoma City. Their friendship means more to me than they could ever know.

Introduction

I rejected Christianity when I was a teen and young adult growing up in the Midwest. My primary understanding of the church came from the noisy, in-your-face fundamentalists who dominated the radio and television airwaves during the decades of the 1960s and '70s. My only other exposure came from my classmates at school who had accepted Jesus as their personal savior. Their insistence that I do likewise did not move me any closer to a relationship with Jesus Christ.

The public face of Christianity led to my exploration of other faiths. From the time I was a teenager I have been a student of the writings of the world's great religious traditions. I am especially indebted to Taoism, Buddhism and Hinduism, and continue to find wisdom and comfort in those Eastern religions. Still, even when I rejected Christianity, I knew in my heart there was something special about Jesus. He had a claim on my life that I could not explain, even as I was often repulsed by the religion that had evolved in his name.

I was in my 30s when I became aware of a strand of

Christianity that hardly resembled the faith I had witnessed over the airwaves and from my "Christian" friends. This progressive Christianity was open-minded, and importantly, it made the claim that Christianity is meant to be a radically inclusive religion. I discovered a Christianity that stands in stark contrast to the fundamentalist version of the faith I had assumed held the church in a stranglehold. Most of the Christians I knew, at least the ones who frequently talked about their faith, were judgmental. Far from espousing an inclusive faith, they seemed to belong to a faith that insisted on turning religion into an exclusive club. You were either in, or you were out. You either believed as they did, or you were going to hell.

After taking the Christian faith seriously as an adult and plumbing it for wisdom and theological depth, I discovered that Anglican theologian W. H. Vanstone was correct when he claimed the church is like a swimming pool, with all the noise coming from the shallow end. I launched out into the deep end of the pool — and have found comfort and nurture there ever since.

I made no major life changes when I was diagnosed with incurable kidney cancer in March 2005. There was no sudden decision to take life seriously while being truly thankful for each and every day. I approached life in that manner long before my diagnosis. And I continue living a life filled with faith, hope and love, surrounded by family and friends.

The story is told that when Henry David Thoreau was on his death bed, his aunt asked him if he had made his peace with God. Thoreau replied, "We've never been at war." I cannot say the same. God and I had our share of battles over the years. The day came, however, when I recognized the futility of fighting with God. I surrendered. And through that surrender my life became complete. I now consider a relationship with God to be the most important aspect of human life.

When I entered the ministry it was not for the purpose of "saving souls." The purpose of my ministry is to point people toward a relationship with God, because I believe the soul of a person who honestly seeks a relationship with God is in good hands.

As I faced the reality of a shorter life than I had expected, the one thing that changed was my preaching. My illness breathed new life into my sermons. I felt a new urgency to speak to the most important matters of faith. My family, my friends and my congregation all took the news of my health problems much worse than did I. I have no fear of death. I trust God without reservation. It seemed important that I convey the reasons for my faith in such a way that others could find comfort when the day inevitably comes that they too must face death.

There is a battle raging in the Christian faith. One side is comprised of fundamentalists who believe in precise and unquestionable answers to our religious questions. The other side is made up of those who reject pat answers and who are willing to live with an element of paradox. I adhere to a liberal, progressive Christianity that is both open minded and inclusive. I reject any form of Christianity in which people are convinced they have secured God in a tidy box of their own making.

Fundamentalism is a threat to Christianity not because of the fundamental beliefs themselves, but rather because of the judgment that so often accompanies those beliefs. For example, it is perfectly acceptable to believe Jesus was born of a virgin. It is not acceptable to think a person who disagrees with you on the subject is going to hell.

For all of its libraries of theological books, Christianity is at heart a fairly simple religion. In fact, the teachings of Jesus can be summarized nicely in four words: *Love everybody. Judge nobody.* To believe that another person is forever beyond the grace of God because of the way that person practices religion is the ultimate judgment. For that reason, modern fundamentalism is often a negative force within the Christian faith.

This book is not an academic work. It is a series of sermons about fundamentalism, which I delivered to my congregation over the course of many Sundays. There is nothing I say in these pages that is not taught in virtually every mainline seminary. Sadly, these thoughts too often fail to make the transition from the classroom to the pulpit.

There are certain authors to whom I am deeply indebted, and the annotated bibliography at the end of this book credits those writers. I opted not to use footnotes, as I edited these sermons from the spoken word to the written word. I preferred these words to flow freely, unfettered and uncomplicated for all readers to comprehend and enjoy.

My prayer is that this book will offer encouragement and hope to those who struggle with their faith. It is okay to wrestle with God! We are commanded to love God with heart, soul and mind. We cannot love God with our mind if we are afraid to think or frightened to ask honest questions.

The human worldview has changed enormously over the course of 2,000 years. When we realized the earth is not the center of the universe, God did not vanish. When we discovered the universe is older than the 6,000 years a literal reading of the Bible would indicate, God did not dissolve into nothingness. And as evolution provides answers to questions regarding the emergence of life on our planet, God is not disappearing. The church is often slow to reconcile its vision of God with the reality God created. But God is indeed the creator of all reality.

We should always remember a great truth that has often been overlooked through the history of our faith: We do not need to protect God from the truth. God is always waiting for us squarely in the middle of any truth we find.

I suggest it is time for Christians to turn away from all the noise and move to the deep end of the pool. The heart of Christianity is alive and well. For all who are willing to dive into the faith and look beneath the surface, God is waiting for us there, bearing the face of Jesus Christ, with a love that is higher, deeper and wider than the furthest limits of our imaginations.

THINK AGAIN

1

The Foundations of Fundamentalism

The word *fundamentalism* evokes an instant response from most Christians. Either they love it, or they loathe it. Either they think it is something essential to the Christian faith, or they think it is the misguided attempt of people with very narrow theologies to impose their religion on the rest of the world.

Before we turn to Christian fundamentalism, we should consider fundamentalism from a wider perspective. Every major religion has fundamentalist followers, that is, people who believe there are certain non-negotiable elements that make their particular religion the one and only worthy religion in the eyes of God. Especially self-righteous and even violent followers have evolved in the monotheistic religions — Judaism, Christianity and Islam.

We see Jewish fundamentalism playing out as a very small minority of modern Jews insist that all of the land claimed by ancient Israel in the Bible should be under Jewish control today. We see Islamic fundamentalism, in its most nightmarish incarnation, encouraging suicide bombers to blow innocent people to pieces, assuring the killer a place of glory in the afterlife. And we see Christian fundamentalism taking over school boards across America as science is trampled beneath the hooves of a fearful and superstitious approach to the Bible.

Amazingly, fundamentalism is a relatively new phenomenon, especially in Christianity. It is true that for as long as humankind has been able to conceive of God, religions have given rise to those who claim sure knowledge of God's will. But what we today call "fundamentalism" actually arose in the late 19th and early 20th centuries, when many sincere people of faith became reactionary, turning away from the realities of the modern world and demanding a return to the perceived good old days of pre-critical thinking about religion.

What happened during that period of time to cause this reaction? Three things are often viewed as the catalysts giving fundamentalism its foundation.

Charles Darwin published *Origin of Species* in 1859, establishing the theory of evolution, and shaking a worldview that had been foundational for centuries of religious belief. People could not reconcile their understanding of the biblical God with a universe that seemed to create itself, a universe that evolved in form, guided by nothing more than explainable natural phenomena. In reaction, some drew lines in the sand regarding the Christian faith. Either you believed in God, or you believed in evolution, but you could not believe in both.

As a Kansan, I am all too familiar with this argument. My congregation and I watch in dismay as the State Board of Education insists high school science classes label evolution as flawed theory. Meanwhile, biblical creationism, parading under the banner of "intelligent design," is advanced as valid science.

Secondly, the advancement of astronomy made it clear that Copernicus and Galileo were right — the Earth is not the center of the universe. Our growing scientific knowledge led to even more uncomfortable conclusions. Our sun isn't the center of the universe. It is just a garden variety star in a universe with more stars than we can humanly imagine. Early in the 20th century we discovered other galaxies. What we had perceived as a vast universe of countless stars was actually only one little galaxy in a universe filled with countless galaxies. Scientists concluded that the universe is much older than the 6,000 years a literal reading of the Bible would indicate. It is especially painful to the human psyche that these discoveries seem to indicate human beings are not nearly as central to the design of the universe as centuries of religious dogma had taught.

The third thing propelling fundamentalism to religious prominence was the outbreak of World War I.

A liberal theology had taken hold of the Christian imagination during and after the Enlightenment. In the 18th century, many Christians turned away from a literal reading of the Bible. Some decided the miracle stories were metaphors and allegories and that God did not actually intercede in the everyday movements of the world. Some questioned what it meant to say Jesus was the Son of God. Many came to believe it was the purpose of humanity to build the kingdom of God here on earth, and that we could do so if we just used the rational minds God gave us and set our hearts to it.

Even those who believed we could build the kingdom of God here on Earth watched in horror as human beings devised more and more efficient ways of killing one another in the 20th century. The carnage of World War I challenged the thinking of those who had placed their hope in the reason of humankind and led many to question the wisdom of trusting human nature. Who could argue with Calvin's assertion that humanity is depraved? Look at the evidence. With its history of violence and warfare, who could still believe that human beings are perfectible through their own efforts? It seemed obvious that human beings are trapped in a fallen world they are incapable of perfecting.

Darwin, astronomy, World War I. So many big questions. So few concrete answers. It was more than many people could take.

This universe is a crazy place. Far too often, it just doesn't seem to make sense. How comforting it would be to have simple answers to life's questions. In the face of confusing science and frightening world events, many people turned to God, or more precisely to a narrow reading of the Bible, seeking a clear set of answers to life's most difficult questions.

That's what fundamentalism does. It provides sure answers to people's questions. In every religion, fundamentalism takes the burden of thinking off the weary shoulders of the followers. The thinking has already been done for you. All you need do is accept the fundamental answers, and then you are in the grace of God. Question the fundamentals, and you surely anger God.

I understand this need, this desire, for solid answers to life's hardest questions. Living in paradox is not something we would necessarily choose, but life is paradoxical. And pretending that life makes perfect sense does not make it so.

The more rabid fundamentalists share a personality trait. They must have answers. It makes little difference their culture or religion. I strongly believe that if our nation's most famous fundamentalist Christians had been born in Saudi Arabia, they would be Islamic fundamentalists. Fundamentalist believers — requiring definitive, unquestionable answers — often turn to the dominant religion of their culture to provide those answers.

So what is the harm in fundamentalism, or at least, what is the harm in Christian fundamentalism? Generally speaking, our Christian fundamentalists aren't blowing people up to make their point. And these people sincerely believe in what they are doing. They feel a real responsibility to convert people to their own way of thinking about religion, because they honestly believe that they are going to heaven and everybody else is going to hell. What's the harm in that?

Here are two examples of why fundamentalism is a negative force in the Christian faith. The first example involves theory, and the second involves the practice of that theory. I derive the theory from the writings of Charles Colson. You may remember that Colson was involved in the Watergate scandal, and he spent time in prison for his actions. It was there that he became a born-again Christian. When released from prison, he started a prison ministry — a ministry that has accomplished much that is good. But let's consider the possible negative impact of his attitude toward religion. In one of his books, *The Body*, Colson explains and defends fundamentalism. He writes:

> A group of theologians, pastors and lay people published a series of volumes titled "The Fundamentals." Published between 1910 and 1915, these booklets defined what had been the non-negotiables of the faith since the Apostles' Creed:
>
> 1. the infallibility of scripture
> 2. the deity of Christ
> 3. the virgin birth and miracles of Christ
> 4. Christ's substitutionary atonement
> 5. Christ's physical resurrection and eventual return
>
> These were then, as they are today, the backbone of orthodox Christianity. If a fundamentalist is a person who affirms these truths, then there are fundamentalists in every denomination — Catholic, Presbyterian, Baptist, Brethren, Methodist, Episcopal... Everyone who believes in the orthodox truths about Jesus Christ — in short, every Christian — is a fundamentalist.

But wait a second! Do you see what he has done? He has defined who is and who is not a Christian. If you do not accept the fundamentals established by those people between 1910 and 1915, then you are not a Christian.

Needless to say, many Christians take exception to this drawing of lines in the sand. Many of us, looking to the example of Jesus and the people he accepted in his ministry, consider Christianity a radically inclusive religion. We find it contrary to the faith to turn Christianity into an exclusive religion, one limited to those who think the right way about theology. That is the theoretical problem many of us have with fundamentalism.

Now consider the real-life implications of putting this fundamental theology into practice. We see one twisted result of that theology every year at Halloween. In fundamental churches all over the country we find an abomination some call "Hell Houses," and others call by a more benign name. Having some personal experience with this, I'll explain how it works.

About 10 years ago, my youngest daughter came running into the house, excited about having been invited to the Halloween party at her best friend's church. No need for a costume, just lots of good wholesome fun. At that time, my wife and I were largely unaware of the way these Halloween parties were orchestrated. I later discovered these parties were a nationwide phenomenon, a tool for inviting our children into the more fundamentalist churches.

It works basically like this: The children of a church invite all their "unchurched" or improperly churched friends to come to the big Halloween party at their church. When the children arrive, they discover that a wing of the church has been turned into a haunted house. What fun! They enter the first dark room, scary music fills the air, and a light suddenly comes on. They see a couple of teenage boys, lying bloody beside their car, each with a can of beer in his hand. An adult voice explains that it is too late for these boys, because they are going to hell. The boys moan in agony, knowing it is too late for them to accept Jesus as their savior and change their fate.

In the next room we find three young girls, apparently within a wall of flame. The room is filled with a foul odor, an effect often created by heating limburger cheese. Each girl cries out that she knew she should not have had an abortion, but now her fate is eternal suffering in the fires of hell. And so it goes. The children are led into a room where a young man finds himself in the presence of the devil, about to be damned for all time. It is explained that he was a great person, who always tried to do the right thing. He gave to charity, he loved his family and friends, he did everything right. But because he had not "accepted Christ as his personal savior," he was doomed to burn for eternity.

After 30 or 40 minutes of this, the shell-shocked children are taken into a room where everything is beautiful and they are given a glimpse of heaven. The music is serene, flowers fill the room with a gentle fragrance, and tasty snacks are available for one and all. They are greeted by the minister or youth minister and told this is a night they will never forget. This is the night they get to choose the destination for their immortal souls. Where will you spend eternity, young man? Now is the time for decision, young lady. Accept Jesus Christ as your personal savior, and you will forever be in the favor of God. Turn away and that decision will haunt you forever.

That is the way a Hell House works. These folks believe in what they are doing, and this is the practical application of their theology. If somebody's child is going to the wrong church, or no church, his soul is in danger. What greater glory could there be than to save some poor 10-year-old who had the misfortune of being born into a family that did not accept your fundamental tenets of the Christian faith?

Now let's return to Charles Colson. He lists five fundamentals, although in a couple of instances he actually puts two fundamentals under a single number. When we look closely at the so-called fundamentals, there are seven:

First, the Bible is incapable of error.

Second, Jesus is fully God.

Third, Jesus was born of a virgin.

Fourth, Jesus performed miracles that defied the laws of nature.

Fifth, one must believe in substitutionary atonement, meaning that we deserve to die for our sins but can live eternally provided we believe Jesus died for our sins.

Sixth, Jesus Christ was physically resurrected from the grave and physically ascended into heaven.

And seventh, Jesus will return again in physical form to judge the living and the dead, bringing about the end of the world.

In chapter two, we will begin an examination of those seven fundamentals, questioning whether this group of teachings really should form the bar by which one is judged to be either a Christian or a heathen. We'll consider what some of the great Christians from the past have said about these seven tenets, these fundamental ideas. And we'll consider the way modern theologians approach these fundamentals.

Let me be clear; it is in no way my intention to belittle fundamentalism. Intensive examination of the Christian fundamentals is a way to survey modern theology in an open-minded attempt to wrestle with, and plumb truth from, our Christian faith.

After a thorough examination of the fundamentals of Christianity, we will seek some new fundamentals — ideas that many of us in the modern church consider the real foundation and the true fundamentals of Christianity.

One word of caution. Those of us who are willing to "take apart" the faith for close examination must be careful not to make the mistake of some over-zealous Christians and start drawing our own lines in the sand. That's the hardest thing of all. How do we keep from being judgmental about people who themselves are judgmental? Even if we decide to take an extremely passive live-and-let-live stand toward our fundamentalist brothers and sisters, what do we do when their kids invite our kids to the big Halloween party at their fundamentalist church?

These are not easy questions, and they don't have simple answers. They are questions we in the modern church must work through together. The situation is not black and white, but rather a paradoxical shade of gray. And that's okay. Many of us think one important role of the church is to help people work through life's paradoxes together.

While the questions life poses are often complicated and heart wrenching, I pray we all find our own ways of surrendering to the love of God. None of us want to be a part of "The Church of Easy Answers." There are enough of those churches.

Together, we commit to enduring and enjoying the struggle, anchored on an honest Christian faith that shapes our lives and the world in which we live.

2

Bible Inerrancy and the Deity of Jesus

We have examined the foundations of fundamentalism and acknowledged that fundamentalism is a phenomenon occurring in every religion. Certain followers in each faith tradition have a need for absolute answers to life's most difficult questions, and they find comfort in the belief that the dominant faith of their culture is the religion favored by God to the exclusion of all others.

As people of faith, we want to be live-and-let-live individuals, but that is sometimes difficult when told we are not Christians unless we believe as the fundamentalists dictate we must. Even the most accepting among us find it hard to deal with fundamentalist believers who approach our children with the hope of "saving" them. However well-intended their actions, in effect their mission is to save our sons and daughters from us, their parents. Fundamentalism calls for a response.

Through the pages of this book, we will seek a Christian response to the fundamentalists' claim of exclusivity by first turning our attention to the seven fundamentals themselves. In this chapter, we will focus on two.

The first fundamental is an idea that many of us find the most untenable of all the fundamentals: The Bible is incapable of error.

The other fundamentals can be accepted through faith, but in order to accept the inerrancy of the Bible, one must look squarely at the truth, yet claim to see something else.

To reject the notion that the Bible is in all cases literally true, we do not have to think the Bible is just another book, a collection of writings with no authority. We can believe the Bible is inspired by God, a source of revelation and the most important book in the history of humanity, and still acknowledge it is not literally true and incapable of error. The truth is simple enough: The books of the Bible were written by human beings. While they were inspired by God, they were still human. And according to the best Christian theology, anything that comes through human beings lacks absolute perfection. God alone is perfect.

The great spiritual truths we find in the pages of the Bible lose much of their meaning when we insist that the Bible is in all cases scientifically and historically accurate. The Bible is filled with great history, but its books are comprised of more than history alone. The Bible contains poetry and allegory, and some of its greatest truths are conveyed through these avenues.

A reasonable person can easily understand that the Bible is neither a literal history book nor a science book. All one need do is read the first two chapters in which we find two very different creation stories. The first story is one of the most powerful, beautiful and meaningful stories ever written, and taken literally it claims that God created the universe in six Earth days. There are countless voices in the modern church telling us we must blindly accept the literal truth of this story, even though it defies the physical truth of the world God has placed all around us.

Because inerrancy of scripture is the first fundamental, fundamentalists claim thinking about this story in anything other than literal terms is to turn away from God. This is where many of us who consider ourselves devoted Christians differ with fundamentalists. We don't have to believe this story is literally, physically, scientifically true to believe the story reveals great and important truth. The ancient writer of that wonderful creation story was truly in touch with the spirit of God. He used his understanding of the world to express some of the most important truths ever expressed. That creation story begins with God saying, "Let there be light," and then lists six days over which God systematically brings forth all of creation.

Consider all the important truths he conveys in that story:

- The universe is not an accident — it was created.
- The universe was created in an orderly and intelligent fashion.
- The process of creation was not instantaneous but happened through time.
- And most importantly, the universe is good, because with each step of the creation process, God calls creation "good."

That creation story is a wonderful way to start the Bible, and it is a wonderful place to start our faith. It teaches that life is not a meaningless accident free of intention and purpose. We are more than meaningless and temporary waves of consciousness in a vast sea of emptiness, the haphazard result of a series of fluke chemical reactions. The author of Genesis 1 believed better, and he said so the best way he knew how. Our faith is not well served by those who claim we must accept literally his ancient view of the physical world in order to accept the beauty and truth of his spiritual message.

Just as we are moved to awed silence by the beauty of the first creation story in chapter one of Genesis, we come to chapter two. And it is almost as if chapter one hadn't been written! We hear the story of creation all over again, but this story isn't anything like the first story. In Genesis 1, God systematically creates everything in the universe and last of all creates a human male and female, at the same time, both in the image of God. In Genesis 2, the first thing

God creates is a man. After that, God creates everything else in creation. Last of all, God decides the man needs a helpmate, and when the man is not impressed by all the animals God has created, God causes the man to go to sleep and from his rib creates a woman. This story line continues in Genesis 3 with the story of the serpent and the forbidden fruit.

Perhaps God reveals in the first two chapters of the Bible the futility of reading the Bible literally. Consider the first creation story. It very clearly states that the last thing God creates is man and woman, at the same time. This is after the vegetation and animals have been created. The second story clearly states that the first thing God creates is a man, then the vegetation and animals, and the last thing God creates is a woman.

Both creation stories are wonderful. The first tells us that the universe is not an accident. It is created. It tells us that human beings are integral, created parts of the universe. The second creation account, the more ancient version, reveals the fallen nature of humanity in relation to God. It too is full of truth and wonderful insights into human nature. However, it is very different from the first story, and it is certainly not science or history. We belittle these stories by thinking they are something other than poetic accounts of the mystery of the universe and of human life in the presence of God. We diminish the lessons and truths of these creation accounts when we insist on their literal interpretation.

After reading just the first two chapters of the Bible, one wonders why any reasonable person would claim the Bible must be read literally. Those two stories are not reconcilable if we insist they are literally factual. The fact is, we can take the Bible seriously, or we can take the Bible literally, but we cannot do both. And those of us who choose to take it seriously have every right to call ourselves Christians.

I will never forget my first week of seminary when one of the professors held up his Bible and asked the students how many thought the Bible was inerrant and therefore incapable of containing any errors. Most of the new students shot up their hands, wanting everybody to know they were true-blue Christians. In response that professor said, "You have just violated the second commandment. You have created a false idol." He went on to explain that in Christian theology, God alone is perfect and incapable of error, and God's perfection has been revealed through Jesus Christ. The Bible is a book existing in time and space, written by human beings. To claim it is infallible is to create a false idol.

One could go through the Bible chapter by chapter and point out problems and inconsistencies, but that is not our purpose. The point is we needn't turn the Bible into a second god in order to grant it great respect. The Bible is the path that leads the human heart to God; but it is not God.

Now we turn to the second fundamental which focuses on the deity of Jesus. This is the idea that Jesus was, and is, fully God. I personally have what theologians call a high Christology. I have an exalted view of the place of Jesus Christ in the eternal scheme of things. But this does not make me a better Christian than those who have a low Christology, a more human view of Jesus.

This second fundamental is all about Christology. Christology asks the question, Who was Jesus? What was his essential nature? The early church had all manner of arguments over this question. Fundamentalists are quick to say their view of Jesus is biblical, and they select the bits and pieces from the gospels that support their views. But the Bible, if read honestly, provides as many questions as answers. For example, in the Gospel of Mark a man kneels before Jesus and addresses him as "good teacher." Jesus instantly replies, "Why do you call me good? No one is good but God alone." Compare that to the Gospel of John where Jesus says, "The Father and I are one. If you have seen me, you have seen the Father."

Let's be honest here. The Gospel of Mark and the Gospel of

John provide very different sketches of Jesus. This means we cannot turn to the Bible alone to figure out the exact nature of Jesus. We must also look to the church, where the faithful have wrestled with Christology from the early days of the faith. In fact, members of the early church spent a lot of time debating the exact nature of Jesus Christ. Was he human? Was he divine? Was he a combination of the two?

Beginning about 300 years after the crucifixion of Jesus, the bishops of the church gathered in a series of councils to determine the true nature of Jesus. From these early church councils came the creeds accepted throughout the church today. The Council of Nicea was convened by the Roman Emperor Constantine in 325 C.E. This council produced the Nicene Creed, the most widely recognized creed and the document that served as the foundation for later creeds. The councils ultimately determined the true nature of Jesus: Jesus is fully human and at the same time fully divine.

Bart Ehrman, an excellent religious scholar from the University of North Carolina, explains in his book *Lost Christianities* that what we now call "heresies" are simply the many ways people thought about Jesus prior to bishops writing those creeds in the fourth and fifth centuries. There were dozens of concepts about who Jesus was and his role in God's universe. All ideas except those developed at the early church councils are to this day considered heresies. For the most part, the church destroyed the writings that disagreed with the bishops' creeds. The writings we have left from the early church provide the narrow thinking of one type of Christianity, which we now call "orthodox" Christianity, orthodox meaning literally "straight thinking" or "right thinking."

Consider some of the heresies that flourished in the early church. The Ebionites believed Jesus was the human son of Mary and Joseph, and that the Spirit of God descended on Jesus when he was baptized. The councils decided: Heresy!

Contrary to the Ebionites, the Marcionites downplayed the

Old Testament, maintaining that the God found in those Old Testament books was not compatible with the God of love and grace preached by Jesus. The God of the Christians was different from the God of the Jews. Again, heretical thinking, according to the councils.

Another group followed what is called Docetism. This was the belief that Jesus was fully divine and only appeared to be human. Some claimed that Jesus was more of an apparition than a real human being. He looked different to everybody who saw him. He did not even leave footprints where he walked! Again, heresy!

Yet another group, the Nestorians, thought that Jesus had two persons within himself, one human and one divine, and he revealed them at different times. Heresy!

In the fourth century, two major schools of thought regarding Jesus became the most popular ways of thinking about his nature. One group of bishops, led by Athanasius, thought Jesus was fully God, of the same substance as God, and that Jesus Christ was uncreated. He cannot be separated from God. The other group, led by Arius, believed Jesus was indeed the Messiah, the Son of God, the Christ. But they believed Jesus Christ was created by God and not the pure substance of God. At the Council of Nicea there was quite a battle, and the followers of Athanasius won. It was determined that Jesus Christ and God were of the same substance, inseparable. Since that time it has been a heresy to think that Jesus Christ was created by God.

At a later council, the Council of Chalcedon, 451 C.E., it was determined that the physical body of Jesus Christ, while he walked the earth, was fully human and fully divine. Jesus was not a homogenous mixture of human and divine, nor was he half human and half divine. He was, paradoxically, fully human and fully divine at the same time. He was one person with two natures. To believe this is to think the right way, to be orthodox. To question this, even today, is technically a heresy, not only in the eyes of traditional fundamentalists, but also in the eyes of most Christian denominations.

Here's the point in all this. Many of us in the modern church feel strongly that it is okay to think about Jesus — to really think about who he was, and what his nature was. Many Christian believers find it possible to believe that Jesus was fully human, created by God, and a great teacher of ethics and wisdom. My personal Christology is a bit higher than that, but this does not make me more Christian than the next person.

Liberal Christians should not claim their views are correct and the fundamentalists' views are wrong. Acceptance of the fundamentals is a matter of faith, and we do not question the way anyone chooses to practice his or her faith. We are even tolerant (although baffled) with those who insist on a literal reading of the Bible. We simply refute the belief that only those adhering to one school of thought have the right to be called Christians.

Good people of faith, from the earliest days of Christianity to the present time, have felt strongly that Christianity is more about a way of life than a strict set of concrete beliefs. May we all grow in our ability and willingness to be a reflection of that way of life as we journey together through this glorious creation.

3

The Virgin Birth and Healing Miracles

Belief in the virgin birth of Jesus is an unquestionable tenet for many who adhere to the Christian faith. It is truly a "sacred cow" of Christianity. What is the foundation of this idea? How important was it to the writers of the gospels and members of the early church?

Scholars' best guess is that Jesus was born sometime in what we now date as the last decade before the common era (B.C.E.). Four B.C.E. and 6 B.C.E. are frequently proposed dates for his birth. We have very little record of his life. In fact, our knowledge is limited to what we find in the Bible, and as we discovered in the preceding chapter, there is more than one way to interpret the Bible.

It is widely acknowledged that Jesus was crucified sometime between 29 and 33 C.E. According to the three synoptic gospels — Matthew, Mark and Luke — Jesus was crucified after a one-year ministry. According to the Gospel of John, Jesus had a three-year ministry. It has long puzzled scholars that nobody made a written account of the life of Jesus until long after his death. The reasons for this are widely debated.

It is assumed that most of his early followers were illiterate, which would account for the delay. More controversial is the idea that Jesus was an eschatological prophet. That is fancy theological language meaning Jesus was preaching about the end of the world. Many scholars believe Jesus' followers were convinced that the end of the world was imminent. There was no time for writing accounts of his life. There was time only for spreading the gospel message and preparing for judgment day. The belief that Jesus' message involved the end of the world has been called into question over the past few decades, but remains one of the explanations for the lack of a written account of his life until long after his death.

The first account of his life was written by the author we now call Mark. The Gospel of Mark was written sometime around 70 C.E., about 40 years after the crucifixion of Jesus. Scholars speculate that the reason somebody finally decided to write such an account was because the followers of Jesus were dying off. Few were left who had actually seen Jesus, who had heard him speak, who remembered his voice and his manner. A record needed to be made for future generations.

What does this first account of the life of Jesus have to say about his birth? Nothing. Literally nothing. In Mark's gospel we meet Jesus as an adult, at the beginning of his ministry, as he is baptized by John the Baptist in the Jordan River. The Holy Spirit of God descends upon Jesus, and a voice from the heavens says, "This is my beloved son, in whom I am well pleased."

Having studied Mark's gospel, two other writers wrote their own accounts of the story of Jesus around 80 C.E. These authors, now called Matthew and Luke, wrote accounts of the miraculous birth of Jesus. Their stories differ in detail, but agree that Jesus was born without the taint of sin. The gospels of Matthew and Luke clearly state that Mary was a virgin when she conceived Jesus through a miraculous act of God.

Finally, the Gospel of John was written at least a decade after the gospels of Matthew and Luke. John's gospel is generally regarded as the most mystical and most misunderstood of the four gospels. Consider the way the story of Jesus evolves from Mark through John: Written first, Mark's gospel begins the story of Jesus when Jesus is an adult. Matthew and Luke, written a decade later, use much of Mark to construct their gospels, but choose to begin their stories with Jesus' conception by the Holy Spirit. The Gospel of John, the final gospel to be written, opens with the beginning of time, the moment of creation. Deliberately echoing the first words of Genesis, John writes, "In the beginning…" and then makes the claim that Jesus Christ was one with God from the moment of creation. It was much later that Jesus became a human being and walked among us. Interestingly, John, like Mark, begins his story of the earthly Jesus not with his birth, but rather with his baptism in the Jordan River by John the Baptist.

Let's sort through this. Matthew, Mark, Luke and John all believed Jesus was the holy Son of God, the Messiah, the Christ. They each believed he was a once-in-the-universe being. He alone is the Son of God.

Did Mark believe Jesus was born of a virgin? Apparently not. Considering he was writing his account to convince people that Jesus Christ was indeed the Son of God, it is odd he failed to mention something as significant as the virgin birth. Did Matthew and Luke believe Jesus was born of a virgin? Yes. That was an important part of their theology. They were convinced of it. Did John, whose gospel does not address the birth of Jesus, believe Jesus was born of a virgin? John has the highest view of Christ to be found anywhere in the Bible. He doesn't blur the line between God and Jesus — he blows the line apart. He places Christ as one with God from the moment of creation, and then has him come into the world to save it. It is hard to imagine that the virgin birth was a part of John's theology, and he simply forgot to mention it.

Paul's letters comprise the bulk of the New Testament. He also has a very high Christology, yet he never once mentions the birth of Jesus, other than to say Jesus was "born of a woman."

Our sources regarding the factuality of the virgin birth, the accounts of Matthew, Mark, Luke, John and Paul, don't seem to agree! Many scholars insist that the virgin birth was an invention of the early church. Because sex was considered naughty, dirty and sinful, Matthew and Luke wanted to depict Jesus as far removed from such earthly sin. Other excellent scholars hold that the virgin birth is an important and non-negotiable tenet of the Christian faith.

For many of us who take Christianity and the Bible very seriously, our stance on this issue is simple. We don't know whether or not Jesus was born of a virgin. Considering the way God seems to work in history, empowering the weak and humbling the strong, it would not be surprising for God to have the Christ appear on earth in the most humble of circumstances, conceived in the normal way and born to an unwed teenager in a political backwater in the ancient world.

However, we recognize that God gets to make the rules. And so here is our stance on the virgin birth: God brought forth the Christ however God wanted to bring forth the Christ. It may have been a miraculous virgin birth, and it may have been a normal birth. The Bible is the only source we have to answer this question, and it offers a mixed witness!

Many liberal thinkers in the modern church remain awed by the notion that Jesus came into the world through a mighty miracle. But if we were to arrive at those metaphorical pearly gates and learn that Jesus was not born of a virgin, it would not damage our faith one iota. Jesus is the Christ. We believe that. How God brought him into the world remains a mystery to us. It is a paradox we choose to live with, rather than trying to convince ourselves we have a sure answer to the question.

Both in my congregation and among the readers of these words there are people who have resolved this issue in their minds. For some, the virgin birth is an important part of their faith. To those people I say, embrace the virgin birth with all your heart. You are in the distinguished company of Matthew and Luke, and God has revealed a truth in your heart that has not been revealed to others.

For others in my congregation and beyond, the virgin birth has always been a stumbling block. They feel they are lesser Christians, because they must pretend they believe something that they don't feel in their hearts is true. To you I say, take that weight off your shoulders. One's view of the virgin birth is not some line in the sand that separates Christian from non-Christian. In fact, John and Paul, with the highest view of Jesus Christ to be found anywhere in the Bible, both seemed unconcerned with the matter. You, too, are in very good company.

What do we do about our fundamentalist friends who insist that belief in the virgin birth is indeed a line in the sand? This is a case where we need to be gentle and respectful. This really is an important tenet for most Christians. Some are more comfortable living with paradox than are others. There is little joy to be found in arguing over religion. And God surely finds no pleasure in seeing people bicker over the virgin birth.

The virgin birth is only the first of many miracles said to have occurred around Jesus of Nazareth. We now turn to fundamental number four: Jesus performed miracles that defied the laws of nature. Broadly speaking, Jesus performs two types of miracles in the gospels. One type of miracle involves healings, both the casting out of demons and physical healings. The second type involves the defiance of the physical laws of nature. In the next chapter we will consider that second type of miracle — miracles that defy the laws of physics. These include such miracles as the miraculous feeding of 5,000 people with the multiplication of the loaves and fishes, the calming of the storm, walking on water and changing water into wine.

For the balance of this chapter, we'll consider the first type of miracle, which involves spiritual and physical healings. Most of Jesus' miracles fall into this category. And most scholars believe that Jesus was indeed a healer. Even many of those who do not believe Jesus was extraordinary in any divine sense still concede that he was a healer — a faith healer.

Consider just one healing story from the gospels. This story is found in the fifth chapter of the Gospel of Mark:

> A large crowd followed him and pressed in on him. Now there was a woman who had been suffering from hemorrhages for twelve years. She had endured much under many physicians, and had spent all that she had; and she was no better, but rather grew worse. She had heard about Jesus and came up behind him in the crowd and touched his cloak, for she said, 'If I but touch his clothes, I will be made well.' Immediately her hemorrhage stopped; and she felt in her body that she was healed of her disease. Immediately aware that power had gone forth from him, Jesus turned about in the crowd and said, 'Who touched my clothes?' And his disciples said to him, 'You see the crowd pressing in on you; how can you say, "Who touched me?"' He looked all around to see who had done it. But the woman, knowing what had happened to her, came in fear and trembling, fell down before him, and told him the whole truth. He said to her, 'Daughter, your faith has made you well; go in peace, and be healed of your disease.'

Today when we envision faith healers, we think of charlatans who take advantage of the gullible by faking cures and bilking people out of their hard-earned money. But faith healing is a reality. Notice what Jesus typically says after he heals a person of an affliction, be it mental, spiritual or physical: "Your faith has made you well." He does not attribute the healing to anything other than the faith of the person who is healed. It seems clear that part of the appeal of Jesus was — and continues to be — due to many people actually being healed in his presence.

In the theology of many of us who take both faith and science very seriously, these are the most important miracles — the healing miracles. They maintain their importance because Jesus is still healing today. That is not to say that a person can be healed in every circumstance if only he or she has enough faith. To think such a thing would be to take the power away from God and put it solely in the hands of the individual. And nobody knows better than a minister that there are times when no amount of fervent prayer and unrestrained faith can bring forth a desired result.

But healing miracles seldom happen unless the element of faith is there. Then they happen all the time. It's not usually as if the sky opens up and the voice of God echoes across creation for all to hear. It is much more subtle than that. A man who has made all the wrong decisions falls to his knees at the homeless shelter, and suddenly there is hope where before there was nothing but despair. A parent who has lost a child wakes up one morning and remembers how to smile. A person plagued with disease finds the inner strength to fight, and the healing begins.

Perhaps you remember what Albert Einstein had to say on the subject of miracles. He once commented that there are basically two types of people in the world: those for whom nothing counts as a miracle and those for whom everything is a miracle. May we all have moments when we see miracles everywhere we look.

4

Miracles: Defying the Laws of Nature

In the first chapter, we examined the phenomenon of fundamentalism from a broad perspective, and in chapters two and three we began looking at each of the fundamentals of Christianity. Having covered the idea of biblical inerrancy and the notion that Jesus Christ was fully human *and* fully divine, we turned to the subject of miracles, starting with the virgin birth and continuing with a brief discussion of the first of two types of miracles performed by Jesus: the healing miracles.

We turn now to the more controversial miracle stories in which Jesus defies the laws of nature. Perhaps the best way to approach this is simply to take a few examples of these miracles and find out what scholars have to say on the subject. Consider the miracle known as the feeding of the multitudes, sometimes called the multiplication of the loaves. Christians should take this story seriously since it is one of the few stories that appears in all four gospels. There is surprisingly little that all four gospels agree on, and evidently this story was a strong part of the memory of each of the originators of the divergent strands of Christianity that emerged in the decades following the crucifixion of Jesus.

The Gospel of Matthew has two stories in which Jesus feeds

the multitudes with only a few loaves of bread and fish. This is the first story from Matthew:

> When he went ashore, he saw a great crowd; and he had compassion for them and cured their sick. When it was evening, the disciples came to him and said, "This is a deserted place, and the hour is now late; send the crowds away so that they may go into the villages and buy food for themselves." Jesus said to them, "They need not go away; you give them something to eat." They replied, "We have nothing here but five loaves and two fish." And he said, "Bring them here to me." Then he ordered the crowds to sit down on the grass. Taking the five loaves and the two fish, he looked up to heaven, and blessed and broke the loaves, and gave them to the disciples, and the disciples gave them to the crowds. And all ate and were filled; and they took up what was left over of the broken pieces, twelve baskets full. And those who ate were about five thousand men, besides women and children.

This simple and straightforward story has caused no shortage of arguments among Bible scholars, who tend to fall into one of four categories regarding the multiplication of the loaves. The first explanation for the story is that it happened exactly as written. This story reveals a miraculous event that actually happened in the life of Jesus. It is not conservative and fundamentalist people alone who believe this. Many open-minded and serious scholars do not think we should try to explain away the miracle stories.

Among those who believe the miracle stories are accounts of historical events, some believe miracles happened at the time of Jesus and continue to happen today. Others believe miracles happened in the ancient world, but no longer occur. In both cases, people believe the biblical miracle stories concerning Jesus should be accepted at face value.

A second explanation for the story of the loaves and fish originated with Albert Schweitzer and is called the sacramental explanation. Schweitzer believed that the meal for the multitudes was something resembling communion. It was a sacramental meal, symbolizing the great banquet in heaven. People did not eat to their fill as far as their stomachs were concerned, no more than we eat to our fill when we celebrate communion today. But they ate to their fill spiritually. Schweitzer believed that the gospel writers, long after the event, transformed it into a miracle story.

A third explanation of this miracle story is called the rationalist explanation. In the ancient world, food was not as abundant as it is today in our modern Western world. The thousands of people following Jesus across the countryside would have been quite aware they could not stop along the road and find food anytime they desired. So they carried food with them, in their knapsacks and in the pockets of their clothing. The rationalist explanation holds that people were shamed into sharing by the words and faith of Jesus. Jesus said there was enough food to feed everybody, and he was right. However, the food was not miraculously multiplied, but rather was produced from the pockets of those present in the crowd as the words of Jesus inspired them to share what they had previously hoarded.

The fourth explanation of this miracle story is the one held by many contemporary Bible scholars. This is the symbolic explanation. Why did the authors of the gospel accounts write their stories? All four of those writers were evangelists. The intentions of Matthew, Mark, Luke and John were to reflect on the life of Jesus in a way that would convince the readers and hearers of their gospel stories that Jesus of Nazareth, the crucified prophet from Galilee, is the long-awaited Messiah. Jesus is the Christ, the Son of God, the redeemer of Israel.

With the symbolic explanation for this story, it is unimportant whether or not the event actually happened. What matters is that the story points to the most important truth in all creation. Jesus of Nazareth is the Christ. And to follow Jesus means one will never need for food, because the follower of Jesus will be fed, both physically and spiritually, now and forever. Since love was at the center of the life and ministry of Jesus, we should always remember that love is the one thing we can give away endlessly — and find ourselves with more than when we started.

Pastors struggle with the correct interpretation of the miraculous multiplication of the loaves and fish. Did it happen as written? Was Schweitzer correct in assuming it was a type of communion meal? Does the rational explanation make the most sense, with people pulling food from their own private stashes to allow for the feeding of the 5,000 individuals? Or is it a symbolic story revealing a truth so important it doesn't matter whether or not it actually happened?

I do not attempt to answer these questions for others. Serious Christians must sort this out for themselves. But individual believers should never insist that the view they accept should become normative for all other Christians. That is where the fundamentalists often go too far, insisting that one either accepts the first explanation, that the story is literal historical fact, or one has no right to be called a Christian. There are good Christians adhering to each of those four explanations.

Let's move on to another miracle story in which Jesus defies the laws of physics: Jesus stills the storm. This miracle is found in the three synoptic gospels, Matthew, Mark and Luke. (John omits most of the miracles from his account.) We'll use Matthew's version of the stilling of the storm, since of all the gospel writers Matthew is the most enamored of the miracle stories. In fact, Matthew has 20 specific miracle narratives in his gospel, and he alludes to, or summarizes, another 14 miracle stories.

This is Matthew's account of the stilling of the storm:

> Now when Jesus saw great crowds around him, he gave orders to go over to the other side of the lake. A scribe then approached and said, "Teacher, I will follow you wherever you go." And Jesus said to him, "Foxes have holes, and birds of the air have nests; but the Son of Man has nowhere to lay his head." Another of his disciples said to him, "Lord, first let me go and bury my father." But Jesus said to him, "Follow me, and let the dead bury their own dead."
>
> And when he got into the boat, his disciples followed him. A windstorm arose on the sea, so great that the boat was being swamped by the waves; but he was asleep. And they went and woke him up, saying, "Lord, save us! We are perishing!" And he said to them, "Why are you afraid, you of little faith?" Then he got up and rebuked the winds and the sea; and there was a dead calm. They were amazed, saying, "What sort of man is this, that even the winds and the sea obey him?"

Once again there is more than one interpretation of this miracle narrative. We can believe it happened exactly as written. We can view the story from a strictly rational perspective and say it was a coincidence that the storm calmed at Jesus' cue. Or we can believe that it is a symbolic story.

The image of Jesus calming the storm is a very important one for me, but I don't know whether or not it depicts a historical event. As Christians, we have our most important answers, and we should be willing to live with paradox regarding other matters. I personally don't mind not having all the answers, as long as I know our loving Creator has the answers. Still, in my faith life and in my more mystical, prayerful moments, Jesus does actually calm that storm on the Sea of Galilee.

Regardless of whether this story is historical or symbolic, we should seek its deeper meaning. Note how the story begins. A scribe, a scholar of that day, claims he will follow Jesus wherever he goes. Jesus warns him that such a claim requires much faith, considering Jesus doesn't know where he will lay down to sleep that night. Another person says he wants to follow Jesus but must first go to his father's funeral. And Jesus says to him, "Follow me, and let the dead bury their own dead."

On the surface, what an offensive thing to say! First, it would be socially unacceptable to avoid the funeral of your father. And second, Jesus seems to indicate that the people who are not following him are just as dead as those whose spirit has departed: Let the dead bury their dead.

Then the true disciples of Jesus follow him into the boat. And what happens when they follow Jesus? Do they live happily ever after? Do they find inner peace? No! They wind up in the middle of a terrible life-threatening storm, and Jesus doesn't even seem to care: He sleeps through the whole thing.

What does this say about following Jesus? It tells us that Jesus does not call people to a life of simple joy and easy living, but rather to a life of discipleship, a life of faith. He is clearly disappointed with his followers when they fear for their lives in the midst of the storm. He says to them, "You of little faith, why are you afraid?" And then he calms the storm.

There is meaning beneath the surface of this miracle, whether or not the miracle happened as written. Perhaps this story tells us that although following Jesus may lead to great trials, we should never forget that Jesus is there if we call on him. Jesus has calmed more than one storm in my life, regardless of what actually happened that night on the Sea of Galilee.

How do we approach these miracle stories? There are countless Bible commentaries with advice for preaching on these stories. The best advice I've found comes from *The New Interpreter's Bible*, which was written by a Bible scholar named Eugene Boring. He provides several suggestions for crafting sermons around the miracle stories. Boring advises clergy to point out that the story has meaning and purpose above and beyond its strict factuality. It's fine to think the story happened as written. Yet even if you don't believe the story is literally true, it is still important and meaningful. Boring also says to avoid using sayings such as "just a story." Stories carry important truths. There is no such thing as "just a story."

According to Boring, it is good to point out the difference in world views between the first century and the modern world. We should remember that the Bible stories were originally written with the belief that we live on a stationary, flat earth, with heaven up in the sky and the realm of death down below. The imagery from those first-century stories must be adapted to make sense to the modern mind.

Boring says to avoid equating belief in the gospel with a particular worldview. And just as important, refrain from making belief in God's presence reliant upon the miraculous. God is present in the everyday details of life, in the beating of our hearts and the love we share with one another. Don't banish God to the realm of the impossible or miraculous.

Eugene Boring is right on target. For many people, belief in the literal historical truth of the biblical miracles is essential to their faith. I certainly have no problem with that. In fact, I am among those who prefer not having the miracles explained away rationally. I believe in letting the stories stand on their own. And I do believe in miracles, particularly healing miracles, because I have witnessed them. They are a mystery to me. I don't understand them. And I resent it when people claim miracles are in the hands of the individual person, if only they have enough faith. Nonsense! Miracles are in the hands of God, and we must accept that God often does not answer our prayers for miracles, regardless of the faith of the person seeking the miracle. Again, Christians must trust God while living with mystery and paradox.

As for the miracles that go beyond healing, stories in which Jesus defies the laws of physics, we must each interpret such stories according to our own conscience. I don't know whether or not Jesus miraculously multiplied a few loaves of bread and a couple of pieces of fish into a feast for 5,000 people. But I do know that out of nothing Jesus can provide the sustenance that will sustain us through this life and through eternity. I don't know if Jesus calmed the storm on that frightening night on the Sea of Galilee. But I do know there is no storm that can accost us in this life — not betrayal, not illness, not even the threat of death itself — that Jesus cannot calm when we turn to him.

So I believe in miracles, in my own way. But as with the other tenets of fundamentalism, I again caution against claiming that such belief separates Christian from non-Christian. Mandatory belief in miracles should not be a required fundamental of the Christian faith. And regardless of our stance on miraculous divine intervention, we should recognize that the difference between heaven and hell, water and wine, a horrible storm and a calm breeze is quite often in the eye of the beholder. We should keep our eyes open for the everyday miracles that are all around us.

5

Substitutionary Atonement

We now turn to substitutionary atonement, the most theologically difficult of all the fundamentals. For many, this complicated idea lies at the very heart of Christianity. All Christians owe it to themselves to wrestle with this idea, even those who have come to reject the theology behind substitutionary atonement.

Substitutionary atonement is the idea that Jesus died for our sins. We hear it from the time we are little children. Jesus died for you. But what does that mean? How does that work? It is an idea that has remained central to Christianity for 2,000 years, but there has been no shortage of arguments about how it works.

Let's begin by looking at the basic concept of atonement. Atonement means, literally, *at-one-ment*. It means to be one with God. How can a human being be one with God? Every religion recognizes that human beings fall short of perfection. If we as Christians accept that there is a Creator of the universe who is pure goodness and beyond all taint of evil, how could any one of us ever be one with that perfect God? For us to even be in contact with such a God would diminish God's perfection.

And so the question remains. How can imperfect human beings be reconciled or atoned with God? To dig deeply into the theology behind this idea, we can't take the easy way out by saying God forgives all our sins, regardless of what evil we have done.

That would mean we have a God who is unconcerned with justice. Think of Dennis Rader, the BTK serial killer responsible for the brutal murders of 10 people in Wichita. Should God give him a free pass? Should such a person's reward be the same as Mother Theresa's? Is there no price to pay for the evil we bring into the world? And although the sins you and I commit fall well short of the transgressions of a serial killer, sin is sin. We all fall short.

Atonement would seem impossible in a just universe. In the early church, atonement was understood through the language of sacrifice. To understand this we must attempt to understand the way Jews practiced their religion during the first century. Jesus and his followers were Jewish. They lived in a thoroughly Jewish world, and they looked at life through a thoroughly Jewish lens.

In that ancient world, there was a way people atoned for their sins. Through the religious practice of sacrifice, people were able to overcome the gap between their sinful selves and perfect God. Faithful Jews traveled to the Jerusalem temple where they offered sacrifices to God. Farmers brought their finest livestock for the priests to sacrifice on the altar in front of the temple. Merchants, craftsman and others who did not raise livestock paid money-changers to purchase an animal for them, and the priests made a sacrifice on their behalf. In the final days of Jesus' life, he entered the temple and overturned the money-changers' tables, claiming the practice of religion had become too commercial. But these men were simply doing their jobs. They were part of the system of commerce that had evolved around the practice of religion.

At the annual festival of Passover, Jews from all over the world arrived at Jerusalem to make their sacrifices. It was at Passover that Jesus caused controversy by overturning the tables of the money-changers. The main task of Pontius Pilate was to keep order and make sure the annual assembly of Jews did not turn into an insurrection against the Roman Empire. He would have been quick to get rid of anybody causing trouble. Not surprisingly, Jesus was crucified shortly thereafter.

According to the Gospel of John, precisely as the priests were slaughtering the Passover sheep on the temple altar, Jesus was crucified. In the theology of the ancient Jews, God's anger at the sins of humanity was appeased when the blood from their best animals flowed down the altar in front of the temple. With this mindset, it was understandable for the followers of Jesus to view him as the ultimate sacrifice to God. If the blood of a sheep could appease God's anger at humanity, how much more would the blood of Jesus Christ, the Messiah, the Son of God, appease His ire?

The writers of the New Testament relied on the language of sacrifice, and it has remained a part of the church for 2,000 years. But what problems that language causes for us in the modern church! We no longer follow a religion in which sacrifice is a recurring ritual. Most of us find it hard to believe that the Creator of the universe holds an anger toward us that is somehow appeased when we kill off our best livestock. And the idea that God would sacrifice his son is very difficult to reconcile with our concept of God. We find the notion of human sacrifice barbaric.

Throughout the first millennium the church accepted the idea of sacrificial atonement without much question. The greatest theologian of the church's first thousand years, St. Augustine, refused to try to explain it in rational terms. He said atonement is a matter of faith seeking understanding and not something that can be rationally explained.

St. Anselm in the 11th century was probably the first person to attempt to explain how substitutionary atonement works. Anselm wrote a book called *Cur Deus Homo* (*Why God Became Man*), in which he claimed the whole problem with atonement was that humankind owed God a debt it could not repay. Nothing a human being could do would overcome the sins he or she had committed in life. And a just God could not forgive sins without some sort of price being paid.

Enter the idea of substitutionary atonement, a way for God to be both forgiving and just. According to the story of Adam and Eve, God did not intend for human beings to have to die. Their disobedience in the Garden of Eden brought death into the world. All of humanity inherited the sin of Adam and Eve. No human being can ever live eternally with God because of humanity's sin. Justice would not permit it.

Humanity owes God a debt it cannot repay. God could forgive that debt, but only by turning away from the idea of justice. So God does the only thing possible to reconcile this situation. God enters the world as a human being and pays that debt. God, living through Jesus Christ, lives a life free of sin, and thus, unlike every other human being who has ever lived, does not deserve to die. But human beings kill this man who is actually God. He dies undeserving, and thus, according to Anselm, God in the form of a human being pays the debt of humanity to himself. Through the death of Jesus on the cross, humanity is reconciled to God. Jesus took our sins upon himself and paid the price for our sins in full.

This is complex and powerful theology. And even St. Anselm agreed with St. Augustine, acknowledging that his rational explanation fell short of truly explaining how Christ died for our sins. Christianity will always be a matter of faith seeking understanding.

The idea of substitutionary atonement has not gone unchallenged over the past thousand years. Modern science certainly calls into question the notion that death was not a part of God's creation prior to the sins of humanity. An evolutionary worldview indicates that all manner of animals, human beings included, experienced death prior to humanity conceiving of, and rebelling against, God.

Early on, many in the church refused to accept the idea of Jesus' crucifixion as some sort of transaction between God and humanity. The two primary theologies that stand in tension with the idea of substitutionary atonement are not lightweight theologies that claim Jesus was a great teacher but nothing more. These theologies hold that humanity falls short of the perfection of God and that through Jesus Christ the gap between humanity and God has been bridged.

First came the theology of Peter Abelard, who lived in the 11th and 12th centuries, just after Anselm. He viewed the life and death of Christ as the ultimate example of God's love. He did not believe in some sort of transaction at the cross that restored the balance between humanity and God. I'll quote Abelard: "The purpose and cause of the incarnation — of God becoming a human being — was that Christ himself might illuminate the world by his wisdom, and excite it to love of himself."

But what about the cross? How is it that millions of people through the ages have fallen to their knees and been changed at their deepest level by envisioning Christ upon the cross? These are the words of Abelard, stating what is now called the exemplary theory of atonement: "Everyone is made more righteous, that is more loving toward God, after the passion of Christ than before, because people are incited to love… And so our redemption is that great love shown for us in the passion of Christ, which not only sets us free from the bondage of sin, but also gains for us the true liberty of the children of God, so that we should fulfill all things not so much through fear as through love."

For Abelard, the example of the cross changes us at the deepest level of our being. The extremely rational theologians of the 19th century, denying the virgin birth, miracles and physical resurrection, took Abelard's views to the extreme. According to them, the only sacrifice involved at the cross was Jesus' sacrifice of himself to make a statement about God's love. Unlike Abelard, they believed Jesus was fully human, in no way divine. According to the rationalists, this man Jesus was so in touch with the love of God that the cross demonstrates the love of God toward us.

Theologians of the 20th century wrestled with different notions of the atonement — the substitutionary view and the exemplary view. And then in 1931 a German theologian named Gustaf Aulen wrote a short book called *Christus Victor*, in which he stated a belief that had been an undercurrent in Christian theology from the beginning. The death of Jesus at the cross was God's victory over evil. God conquered evil through Jesus not by bashing it over the head but, rather, by entering into the very heart of evil and never losing his love.

Gustaf Aulen's view of the atonement is often called the triumphant view. God triumphed over evil, over death itself, through the cross. The death and resurrection of Jesus was the ultimate victory of God over the forces of evil. For Aulen this was an objective victory, an event that took place at a particular time and place in history. Two of the greatest theologians of the 20th century, Rudolf Bultmann and Paul Tillich, expounded on the writings of Aulen and turned them into something very different.

Attempting to demythologize the New Testament, Bultmann claimed the victory of God at the cross was a victory over unbelief and inauthentic existence. And Paul Tillich reworked Aulen's theories to claim the victory of Christ on the cross to be a victory over the existential forces that deprive us of a full, happy authentic life. Bultmann and Tillich took Aulen's objective view of the cross and turned it into something subjective, something deep within the consciousness of human beings. This is significant because suddenly the life, death and resurrection of Christ aren't actual happenings of 2,000 years ago so much as concepts that can have important effects inside each of us today. Jesus' death and resurrection turns death back into life, and takes us along for the ride, not on a hill outside Jerusalem in the distant past but right here, right now, deep within each of us.

Some modern fundamentalists claim that our atonement with God is possible only through the shedding of Jesus' blood. Had Jesus been killed in some other way, atonement would not have happened. Just as the blood of those animals in first-century Israel had to flow down the altar to justify us in the eyes of God, the blood of Jesus must flow down the cross to wash away our sins.

For many in the modern church, such sacrificial language leaves us more confused than inspired. Yet we understand that there is something unique, something special, about the death of Jesus. So we wrestle with how it works, and we struggle with what it means to say "Jesus died for our sins."

I suggest we draw no lines in the sand to separate Christians from one another. I personally agree with St. Augustine that there are times when our faith has to take the lead. Something happened at the cross. Millions of people over the centuries have been changed by contemplating Jesus on the cross. I cannot believe the crucifixion was simply an unfortunate and tragic end to the life of a great man.

I can honestly say I am a different person because Jesus Christ was crucified. But I have no logical words to fully explain how that event has affected my life. We read the words from the Gospel of John, perhaps the most famous words in the Bible: "For God so loved the world that he gave his only Son, so that everyone who believes in him may not perish but may have eternal life." And there is something there that rings true in our hearts.

I wrestle with that passage time and time again. I have come to believe the cross is even more powerful than that. I believe all evil was conquered at the cross. I don't think it is simply a matter of belief in Jesus. I believe this whole mess of a world was reconciled to God at the cross. Because of this, I have a high Christology, a more elevated view of Jesus, than the fundamentalists. I honestly believe God has covered all the bases. It is not a matter of what we think, or believe, or confess. God's love has taken care of everything, and we see that love at the cross.

God truly loves us. And somehow, some way, we can see God's love when we look at Jesus. Believing that alone is more than enough to make us Christians.

6

The Physical Resurrection

As we look back at the origins of our faith, it is doubtful that Christianity would have grown into the world's largest religion if not for the early church's belief in the resurrection of Jesus. At the heart of our faith is the claim: Christ is risen! This belief gave the early martyrs of the church the courage to stand up to their oppressors, to face ugly and painful deaths at the hands of those who asked them to renounce their faith.

What leads to such faith? What compels a person to face death fearlessly, preferring death to a life in which he or she has turned away from Jesus Christ? What is the source of such unshakable belief? The answer, quite simply, is experience. The founders of the early church experienced Jesus Christ after his death. Something real happened that they could not ignore, something so powerful and life-changing they were willing to lose everything in order to serve the Risen Christ of their experience.

As I attempt to discuss the resurrection of Jesus, I should acknowledge my personal perspective. I believe in the resurrection. I believe it happened. I think it was real. But just as surely as I am convinced in the truth of the resurrection, I must admit that I have serious reservations about the physical resurrection. I am not convinced that the resurrection had anything to do with the atoms, molecules and cells that comprised the earthly body of Jesus of

Nazareth.

Our sources in searching for the truth of the resurrection are the four gospels and the writings of Paul. Each of the gospels contains accounts of the post-resurrection Jesus speaking with the disciples. While the accounts differ in detail, there are eight times, spread among the four gospels, when Jesus makes post-resurrection appearances. Jesus appearing to the women who had visited his tomb is included in all four gospels. Other stories about his post-resurrection appearances are found in either one, two or three of the gospels.

Although the reported details vary, one thing is certain. The writers of the gospels very much believed that Jesus Christ lived on after his crucifixion. They believed that God, through a mighty miracle, had overcome death itself through Jesus. To read their stories, it certainly appears that Jesus was there in physical form. On different occasions he talks with them, walks with them, eats with them. Jesus even has Thomas place a hand in his pierced side so Thomas will know that Jesus is real.

Still, it is mysterious how Jesus arrives and departs. He suddenly appears to his disciples even though they are in a room with locked doors and windows. He breaks a loaf of bread in front of two of his followers, and suddenly vanishes. The gospel writers are intent on convincing the reader that this Risen Christ was real, that he was physically there with them. But he didn't behave like a person who had walked out of his grave. This Jesus wasn't resuscitated; he was resurrected, and there seems to be a difference between resuscitation and resurrection that is nearly impossible to explain.

In attempting to understand the nature of the resurrection, we have the writings of Paul to go along with the four gospels. Paul never met Jesus of Nazareth. It was Paul's job to round up and persecute the followers of this crazy new sect of Judaism, which had developed around the crucified Jesus. Paul learned of a new group of Jesus' followers in Damascus and was on his way there when he experienced the Risen Christ. His experience was so powerful, Paul became the first great evangelist, starting churches all over the Middle East, Asia and Europe. Paul addresses the resurrection with great directness in his first letter to the Corinthians. The following is from the 15th chapter of 1st Corinthians:

> But someone will ask, 'How are the dead raised? With what kind of body do they come?' Fool! What you sow does not come to life unless it dies. And as for what you sow, you do not sow the body that is to be, but a bare seed, perhaps of wheat or of some other grain. But God gives it a body as he has chosen… There are both heavenly bodies and earthly bodies, but the glory of the heavenly is one thing, and that of the earthly is another. What is sown is perishable, what is raised is imperishable… It is sown a physical body, it is raised a spiritual body. If there is a physical body, there is also a spiritual body... What I am saying, brothers and sisters, is this: flesh and blood cannot inherit the kingdom of God, nor does the perishable inherit the imperishable.

For Paul it seems clear that the resurrection is something spiritual as opposed to something physical. The problem many have with the idea of a spiritual resurrection is that they think in materialistic terms. For something to be real, it must exist physically. It must have a material body. For something to be real, it must be a measurable part of the empirical universe.

But consider, for example, love. We can see the results of love, but we cannot see love itself. Is love real? Pour out a cup of love so we can weigh it, measure it. Drop off some love in my church mailbox so I can show it to the rest of the congregation. Something can be real without being empirically measurable. Unless we begin our discussion of the resurrection with that truth in mind, we will never be able to differentiate between resurrection and resuscitation.

The Bible gives us mixed signals regarding the resurrection. What have modern theologians said about the resurrection? Is the resurrection physical? Spiritual? What are we to make of these seemingly contradictory stories from the Bible? There is a great deal of disagreement over the nature of the resurrection, even among scholars. We'll briefly consider four modern theories.

First is the enlightenment view espoused by G. E. Lessing. For Lessing, the resurrection simply did not happen. Jesus walked the earth as a human being. Human beings die, and their bodies turn back to dust. That's just the way it is. With this purely rational approach, the resurrection is simply another Bible miracle that did not really happen. Lessing insisted that it does not make sense to accept eye-witness accounts from the distant past when those accounts are contradicted by present-day experience.

A second approach treats the resurrection as a myth. This idea is attributed to 19th-century theologian David Friedrich Strauss, who was very much a rational thinker. Claiming there could be no historic fact behind the resurrection, he thought that the Risen Christ was an idea, a concept in the subjective mind of the believer. For those who accepted Strauss's theory, Christianity became a religion dedicated to remembering the dead Jesus, as opposed to celebrating the Risen Christ.

A third approach comes from one of the great 20th-century theologians, Rudolf Bultmann. He also refused to believe in miracles, but claimed that the resurrection happened as an event in the lives of the disciples. The Risen Christ lives not as a physical being, a resuscitated Jesus, but rather in the hearts of his followers. This may at first sound the same as Strauss's view, but there is a major difference. Strauss attempted to turn Christianity into a religion about the dead Jesus. Bultmann still centered the Christian faith on the Risen Christ, believing that Jesus Christ truly lives on through his followers.

Finally we come to Karl Barth, the most influential theologian of the 20th century. Barth claimed that the resurrection of Jesus is a historical fact. Period. That tomb was empty because Jesus Christ was resurrected. It was both physical and spiritual. It happened. And understanding that is purely a matter of faith.

At this point, you may be thinking, "This is too much information. I don't know what to believe." Although I have questions about whether or not the resurrection involved the actual body of Jesus, I am a believer in the resurrection. I can't lay out some logical argument as to why I believe in the resurrection, so I will discuss it from a personal level.

With regard to the resurrection, the stumbling block for me has always been what ultimately happened to the body of Jesus. If Jesus appeared to his disciples in physical form, if his body was resuscitated, what ultimately happened to that body? Why isn't he still walking around on earth today? Matthew and John do not address that issue. Mark and Luke do address the issue. Their answer is that Jesus ascended into heaven. Mark writes, "So then the Lord Jesus, after he had spoken to them, was taken up into heaven and sat down at the right hand of God." Luke writes, "While he was blessing them, he withdrew from them and was carried up into heaven."

During the first century, the people of Israel believed in a three-tiered universe. Human beings lived on a stationary, flat earth. The realm of death existed below. Heaven was above. And God was up there in the sky. So following his death and resurrection, Jesus ascended into the sky to be with God. The problem is obvious. If Jesus physically ascended into the sky, where is he now? Science tells us if Jesus traveled as fast as a physical entity could possibly travel, he is still somewhere in the Milky Way galaxy. It is difficult to accept the literal truth behind the ascension of Jesus with our modern worldview.

Personally, the story makes sense to me only if I think not in terms of earth being "down here" and heaven "up there," but rather in terms of the physical and the spiritual. Through the resurrection, Jesus changed from the physical Jesus of Nazareth into the spiritual Christ. And that spiritual Christ is not bound by the laws of physics. The Risen Christ is a spiritual reality that transcends time and space.

Does the Risen Christ exist physically? I would not deny that God has the power to make it so. But if Jesus lives on today in some physical form, say on some planet circling some nearby star, what has that to do with my life? The Christ of my experience, the Christ I meet in prayer, the Christ who is present when two or more are gathered in his name, the Christ who inspires people to noble deeds and acts of kindness, that Christ is not physical. That Christ is spiritual, and he lives, truly and actually, in the hearts and minds of his followers.

The Risen Christ is real. He lives as more than a memory. Jesus is real enough to have thousands of people face martyrdom rather than renounce him. Real enough to have believers build countless churches all over the world in which to worship Christ. Real enough to have broken through the walls of pain and anguish in which millions of people have entrapped themselves, giving hope for a new and better life.

Let's relate all this back to fundamentalism. Fundamentalism insists that one must believe in the physical resurrection and the physical ascension of Jesus into the heavens in order to be a Christian. I refuse to accept this. In fact, even though I personally have a strong belief in the reality of the resurrection (not as a physical reality but rather as a spiritual reality), I also believe that the rationalist thinkers, who do not believe in the resurrection in any way, still have a right to be called Christians.

If people attempt to shape their lives according to the teachings of Jesus, that makes them Christians. It is interesting that the early followers of Jesus called themselves "The Way." They distinguished themselves from others by the way they lived their lives. They loved one another, they cared for the poor, they tended to the sick, and they were committed to living good and faithful lives.

The resurrection of Christ is a central tenet for most Christians. Are we to argue over the resurrection with our fundamentalist friends? I don't think so. In fact, the death and resurrection of Jesus is too important an issue to bicker over. I don't know exactly what happened between Good Friday and Easter, but something very powerful did take place. People should allow others to embrace that event freely and openly in a manner that honors individual belief.

That event, the cross, the death, the resurrection, however we perceive it, has affected millions of people over the centuries. It has changed people. That event reaches across the ages, giving strength and hope to those who have fallen into despair. Psychologist Rollo May wrote, "Humans are the strangest of all God's creatures, because they run fastest when they have lost their way." I believe that when we find ourselves lost and running aimlessly and finally realize that we cannot run forever, the best place to stop is at the foot of the cross. What awaits us there is beyond the wildest limits of our imaginations. We find there a love that ends our need for running, because it is there that Good Friday turns into Easter. It is there that good conquers evil, light overcomes darkness, and time and eternity intersect. At the cross, we move from death to life and into the heart of God.

7

The Second Coming

We now move to the seventh and last of the fundamentals: the Second Coming. For fundamentalists, the Second Coming of Christ means the physical return of Jesus, who will appear from the sky in order to bring about the end of the world as we know it. Fundamentalist ideas regarding what will happen at the end-times are taken largely from the Book of Revelation, which we will focus on in the next two chapters. In this chapter, we will examine the gospels and discover what they have to say about the Second Coming.

Matthew, Mark and Luke have a great deal in common regarding what will happen at the end of the world. When you put those three gospels side by side and study the passages that deal with the end of the world and the Second Coming, they track almost perfectly. Students of the Bible know that most scholars agree that Mark's account was the first to be written, sometime around 70 C.E. Matthew and Luke wrote their accounts after having read Mark's. For this discussion, we will use Mark's gospel as our guide.

To begin with, it is helpful to understand a few theological words: *parousia*, *eschatology* and *apocalypse*. *Parousia* is a Greek word meaning "coming" or "arrival," and theologians use it to refer to the Second Coming of Christ. The whole broad notion of Christ's Second Coming and how that relates to "last things" is summarized in the word *parousia*. *Eschatology* is the word used for the branch of theology that deals with last things as they relate to eternal life, heaven and hell. And the word *apocalypse* refers to a sudden revelation of God. We'll deal with that word when we turn to the Book of Revelation, which is written in a style called apocalyptic literature.

Although I attempt to refrain from using theologically technical language in this work, those three words are integral to a discussion of the Second Coming, and the reader whose interest is peaked enough to delve further into the subject will find the words used with great frequency.

The words Mark attributes to Jesus regarding the end-times are found in Mark 13, a chapter many theologians call "the little apocalypse." Scholars argue about whether or not Jesus actually said the things attributed to him in this passage. Many believe these are Mark's words, posthumously placed in the mouth of Jesus of Nazareth in order to embolden a church that was facing great persecution. At the time of this writing, around 70 C.E., the crucifixion of Jesus was about 40 years in the past. At that time, Christians were being dragged before councils and beaten in some of the synagogues. They were widely hated and persecuted.

Looking back on the life of Jesus while writing for his contemporary audience, Mark has Jesus say this: "…they will deliver you up to councils; and you will be beaten in the synagogues; and you will stand before governors and kings for my sake, to bear testimony before them. And the gospel first must be preached to all nations. And when they bring you to trial and deliver you up, do not be anxious beforehand what you are to say; but say whatever is given you in that hour, for it is not you who speak, but the Holy Spirit… You will be hated by all for my name's sake. But he who endures to the end will be saved."

Such words surely gave courage and strength to those facing persecution long after Jesus' death, whether Jesus actually spoke them or not. We will go through the passage without engaging in the scholars' debate about its authenticity.

Mark 13 begins with Jesus foretelling the destruction of the temple, something that would happen at about the time Mark wrote his gospel 40 years in the future. Jesus says, "There will not be left here one stone upon another." The disciples then ask Jesus about the end-times, and what signs may appear to warn people the end is near.

Jesus says, "Take heed that no one leads you astray. Many will come in my name, saying, 'I am the Christ,' and they will lead many astray. And when you hear of wars and rumors of wars, do not be alarmed; this must take place, but the end is not yet." Jesus then tells the disciples of the persecutions we have already mentioned and adds, "If anyone says to you, 'Look, here is the Christ!' or 'Look, there he is!' do not believe it. False Christians and false prophets will show signs and wonders, to lead astray, if possible, the elect. But take heed; I have told you all things beforehand."

Jesus then says that when the end times come it will be obvious, for there will be "such tribulation as has not been from the beginning of the creation which God created until now, and never will be."

And now, we arrive at Mark's version of the Second Coming:

> But in those days, after that suffering, the sun will be darkened, and the moon will not give its light, and the stars will be falling from heaven, and the powers in the heavens will be shaken. Then they will see the Son of Man coming in clouds with great power and glory. Then he will send out the angels, and gather his elect from the four winds, from the ends of the earth to the ends of heaven.
>
> From the fig tree learn its lesson: as soon as its branch becomes tender and puts forth its leaves, you

> know that summer is near. So also, when you see these things taking place, you know that he is near, at the very gates. Truly I tell you, this generation will not pass away until all these things have taken place. Heaven and earth will pass away, but my words will not pass away.
>
> But about that day or hour no one knows, neither the angels in heaven, nor the Son, but only the Father. Beware, keep alert; for you do not know when the time will come. It is like a man going on a journey, when he leaves home and puts his slaves in charge, each with his work, and commands the doorkeeper to be on the watch. Therefore, keep awake — for you do not know when the master of the house will come, in the evening, or at midnight, or at cockcrow, or at dawn, or else he may find you asleep when he comes suddenly. And what I say to you I say to all: Keep awake.

A couple of points should be made. First, Jesus clearly states that no one knows when the end will come, "neither the angels, nor the Son, but only the Father." So we should not get too worried when we hear somebody claiming they have studied scripture, decoded its message and determined the date for the end of the world.

Second, notice that Jesus says, "This generation will not pass away until these things have taken place." How do we deal with that? Many scholars think those words of Jesus are why no account of his life was written for so long after his death. There was no need to leave a written copy of Jesus' teachings for future generations, because Jesus had promised to return in their lifetimes. Clearly, that did not happen. Or did it? Could there have been a giant misunderstanding about what Jesus was trying to say?

The Book of Acts, which reveals what happens to the disciples after the crucifixion of Jesus, claims that a little less than two months after the death of Jesus the Holy Spirit of God descends upon them. This is what we today call Pentecost. The gospels tell us that Jesus promised to send a helper to the disciples after his death. Could this arrival of the Holy Spirit in their lives have been the Second Coming he was talking about? Classical Christian theology holds we have one God comprised of three persons: Father, Son and Holy Spirit. One could easily argue that the arrival of the Holy Spirit at Pentecost was indeed the Second Coming.

Another way of looking at the stories of the Second Coming and "last things" is that each and every human being will indeed reach the end at some point. We are not eternal. We are mortal. From a cosmic perspective, the end of each of our worlds is not that far in the future. Part of Christian hope is the notion that the end of our days is not truly the end. Figuratively speaking, we hope to see the sky open up and Jesus coming to us on the clouds of heaven.

Fundamentalists, in many cases, have latched on to the phrase, "The Son of Man [will come] in clouds with great power and glory." But many believe this is one of those cases where we must take into account the worldview of those first century authors. Just as the claim was made that following his death Jesus ascended through the sky to be with God, so it is with his Second Coming. He comes out of the sky. In that ancient worldview, God was up in the sky. So of course that is from whence the Messiah originally came, the place to which he returned after his resurrection and the place from which he will return to earth at his Second Coming.

In chapter four we discussed Bible scholar Eugene Boring. He advises against several things when discussing the miraculous stories of the Bible. First, we should never associate the presence of God purely with the miraculous. God is in the details of life at least as much as the miraculous exceptions. Boring also warns against forcing an ancient worldview on the modern Christian. And that is what we do when we think literally about the Second Coming of Jesus from the clouds above. In God's miraculous universe, Jesus may well have departed in a miraculous fashion, and he may indeed return; but we needn't force our thinking on that subject into a first-century worldview. This is the age of quantum physics. Our greatest scientists have blurred the line between mind and body, between the physical and the spiritual. We don't need to force our theology into a first-century view of reality.

I will conclude this discussion of the Second Coming by turning to modern theological arguments regarding "last things." Most theologians today do not envision the Second Coming as the physical return of Jesus from the skies above. Some argue that just as the first coming of Jesus was not what anybody expected, the Second Coming will be (or was) unlike anything we expect. Remember the first coming. The awaited Messiah was supposed to be a warrior. He was supposed to return Israel to the glory days of King David, conquering all Israel's enemies with his mighty sword. But the Messiah turned out to be something completely different, a man who saved the world not through the power of the sword but rather through the agony of the cross.

Perhaps the Second Coming will also be different from our expectations. Some claim the Second Coming occurred during Pentecost, when the Holy Spirit came into the world. Many believe that as the spirit of Christ covers the earth through the hearts of believing Christians, that is the Second Coming. In other words, the church, also called the Body of Christ, is the Second Coming.

Others take a more eschatological view of the Second Coming, believing it does indeed have to do with the end of the world, but insist we must read the biblical accounts figuratively. Modern science has not made the universe less mysterious. The universe just keeps getting stranger and stranger as our knowledge increases. For a first-century Jew, the best way to envision the relationship between Jesus and God was to think of Jesus on the earth and God in the sky. Then came Copernicus and Galileo, and it was no longer reasonable to think we live in a three-tiered universe, with God above and death below and we human beings between the two on a flat and stationary earth.

Newton did the math and we thought we had things figured out. Then Einstein proved that the scientific worldview of the Enlightenment was off the mark. Physical masses and time are not the foundations of the universe. In fact, mass and energy cannot be separated from the viewpoint of physics. And according to Einstein, time is pretty much in the eye of the beholder, with the speed of light being the only constant we have to work with. Time is part of an expanding and contracting time-space continuum.

And even Einstein was completely confused by the emergence of quantum physics. Our four-dimensional universe, the universe we understand, the universe of height, width, depth and time, is only a small part of the picture. Quantum physicists now debate whether there are 10, 11 or 26 dimensions. Whatever the number, concepts such as up and down, left and right, even before and after can lose their meaning within this strange "new" quantum world.

In the face of such mystery, how do we deal with concepts such as the ascension of Jesus into the sky and his physical return from the clouds? How do we deal with ideas such as the end of time in a universe where time cannot be said to exist outside of a conscious mind? The answer given by some in the modern church is to leap 2,000 years into the past and reclaim the worldview of those who lived in the first century. And that is understandable. This universe can be a scary and confusing place.

The answer for most serious theologians is to fall to their knees in awe at the wonder of the universe and the amazing glory of the God who called it into being and who holds it together moment to moment. In awed silence we recognize that our theological concepts, concepts such as the Second Coming, are a mystery to be embraced rather than a strict creed to be understood in a particular way.

The only thing we know for certain is that every time we human beings think we have figured out the universe, we soon discover we are wrong. That should humble us. And amazingly, as we learn and grow, we seem to get smaller and smaller, and God keeps getting bigger and bigger. It is hard enough to imagine a God who over a period of six days creates a planet, puts people on it and surrounds it with a sun, moon, planets and stars. How much more amazing, how much more glorious, how much more unfathomable is the God who creates a universe that is billions of years old with billions of galaxies, the God who creates a multidimensional universe and reveals to our senses only four dimensions so we can try to make some sense of things.

That is the God we've got. When we try to use words to describe the power of God, we start sounding strange. We might start talking of miraculous births and miracles and resurrections, and all these are ways of embracing the mystery of life in the presence of such a God. But they should not be ways of defining and limiting God, of forcing God into a box we can easily understand and control.

In chapters eight and nine we turn to the Book of Revelation, a book many fundamentalists view as the most important book of the Bible, believing it provides a literal foretelling of the end of the world. It is here that most of the theologies involving "last things" and the Second Coming have their foundation. In our examination of this book, we will discover a Jesus very unlike the one who walked the earth 2,000 years ago. In fact, some have observed that those who are obsessed with the Second Coming of Jesus are often people who don't care much for the Jesus we got the first time. They would have preferred an angry warrior to a loving savior. We get our angry warrior in Revelation.

That is a terrible thing to do to Jesus! We should always remember that God, who created this mysterious universe with all its galaxies and all its dimensions, longs to be in relationship with each and every one of us.

And although we cannot begin to understand the mystery of God, we can recognize God's nature. It is there in Jesus Christ. May he live in our hearts every second of our lives.

8

Marcus Borg's Overview of The Revelation of John

Having examined the seven basic ideas that form the foundation for modern fundamentalism, we now turn to the biblical book that serves as the foundation for much of the fundamentalist view regarding the coming end of the world. Revelation is the most misunderstood book of the Bible. New Testament scholar Marcus Borg wrote a marvelous book entitled *Reading the Bible Again for the First Time.* This book includes the finest overview of Revelation that I have ever discovered. In the coming pages, I will provide an overview of Revelation, an overview that relies heavily on Borg's work. I will be using his writing for both the outline of my presentation and the bulk of its content.

We must first consider who wrote The Revelation of John and how it has been viewed over the ages. We'll examine the amazing story and the mind-boggling series of visions found in the book. Then in chapter nine, we will look at two very different ways in which the book can be approached, the two interpretations of Revelation we find in the world today. But we can't attempt to interpret all the wild stuff going on in Revelation if we don't read over the story first.

The word *revelation* is a translation of the Greek word *apoca-*

lypse. The words are synonyms. The person who wrote this book was named John. So the full title of the book is written one of two ways: The Revelation of John or The Apocalypse of John.

Apocalypse is defined as "an unveiling" or a "revelation." There is a style of writing called apocalyptic literature that was popular over a 300-year period, from about 200 B.C.E to 100 C.E. Borg points out that apocalyptic literature deals with mysterious symbols, heavenly futures, numbers with secret meanings, evil powers being overthrown by God, amazing beasts described in great detail, intense suffering and catastrophes of epic proportions. Along with Revelation, the Old Testament Book of Daniel is the other biblical writing that fits into this category.

Revelation is positioned as the last book of the New Testament, and thus, at the end of the Bible. It wasn't the last book of the Bible to be written, and the person who wrote it certainly had no clue that his work would one day wind up at the end of the Christian canon. Its location in the Bible is due to its subject matter: the end of the world. The Bible begins with the words "in the beginning" and concludes with a book about how everything ends, with God's judgment on the world and the Second Coming of Christ.

Authors Hal Lindsay, Tim LaHaye and others of a fundamentalist bent have used Revelation to scare people into the faith. I view this as the absolute lowest from of evangelism and a perversion of the Christian message. Many serious Christians through the ages have wished this book had never been included in the Bible. And it almost wasn't. As the theologians of the early church debated about what writings would be included in the official Christian Bible and what writings would be left out, the book of Revelation generated the most heated debate.

Even 1,000 years after the Christian canon was closed, many Protestant reformers, including Martin Luther, John Calvin and Ulrich Zwingli, held the Revelation of John in very low regard. Luther felt it maintained a secondary stature among the books of the Bible and said he personally wished it could be thrown into the Elbe River. Zwingli refused to accept it as a part of the Bible. And Calvin wrote in-depth commentaries on every book of the New Testament, with the exception of Revelation, which he simply chose to ignore.

The author of Revelation, known simply as John, lived off the coast of modern-day Turkey on the island of Patmos. The claim that this is the same John who wrote the fourth gospel is rejected by almost all modern scholars. The John who authored the book of Revelation most likely wrote it around the year 95 C.E., although a minority of Bible scholars argue that it was written earlier, in the 60s, during the reign of the Roman emperor Nero.

The number 666, the sign of the beast and the number of the antichrist, has modern-day prophets of doom continually on the lookout for the hidden meaning of the number so they will be able to recognize the antichrist when he rises up to take over the world. But the number 666, using the rules of an ancient coding method called "gematria," is translated "Caesar Nero." And most modern scholars insist that if you want to find the person to whom the number 666 refers, you needn't look to the future for some antichrist. You should rather look 2,000 years in the past to the emperor of Rome.

We'll examine more of the symbolism of Revelation in chapter nine. But first, we must attempt to recap the whole book from start to end. As we begin that process, I emphasize that there are two very different ways to read this book. While these two ways of approaching the book of Revelation will be covered in depth in the next chapter, it is beneficial to have some idea of the different approaches before we summarize the book.

One approach is to view this book as one man's amazing vision of the future, a vision that is literally true because it is found in the Bible. The other approach is to view this book as one man's symbolic examination of the world in which he lived. The way one chooses to approach this story makes all the difference in the world; in fact, it reads like two completely different stories, depending on which approach you take. Is this a story about the future of our world today, or is it a story about a world 2,000 years in the past? For the time being, we'll turn to the Revelation of John, and let the story speak for itself.

The Book of Revelation is a letter, inspired by a series of visions, written by John of Patmos to the seven churches in Asia. John writes, "I was in the spirit on the Lord's day, and I heard behind me a loud voice like a trumpet saying, 'Write in a book what you see, and send it to the seven churches, to Ephesus, to Smyrna, to Pergamum, to Thyatira, to Sardis, to Philadelphia, and to Laodicea.'"

When John turns to see who is speaking to him, he sees the Risen Christ. The way he describes what he sees is typical of the heavy symbolism and rich imagery of apocalyptic literature:

> Then I turned to see whose voice it was that spoke to me, and on turning I saw seven golden lampstands, and in the midst of the lampstands I saw one like the son of Man, clothed with a long robe and with a sash across his chest. His head and his hair were white as snow; his eyes were like a flame of fire, his feet were like burnished bronze, refined as in a furnace, and his voice like the sound of many waters. In his right hand he held seven stars, and from his mouth came a sharp two-edged sword, and his face was like the sun shining with full force.

According to the story, John faints dead away when he sees all this (as one might imagine he would). After John regains consciousness, this amazing figure, which represents the Risen Christ, concludes John's first vision by saying, "Now write what you have seen, what is, and what is to take place after this. As for the mystery of the seven stars that you saw in my right hand, and the seven gold lampstands: the seven stars are the angels of the seven churches, and the seven lampstands are the seven churches."

Visions, imagery, symbolic numbers — all the elements of apocalyptic literature are present in that first vision of John. Throughout the book, John uses the words "I saw" to preface each vision — and he uses the words "I saw" more than 50 times.

In Revelation, the number seven keeps appearing. In biblical literature, seven is a number that symbolizes perfection. The first vision contains seven stars, seven lampstands and seven churches. Future visions have seven letters, seven seals, seven bowls and seven trumpets. And the book is constructed with seven beatitudes, seven hymns, seven categories of people, seven references to the altar and seven proclamations of the Second Coming of Christ. As you can see, Revelation is filled with symbolism. Perhaps this should warn us of the danger of reading it literally instead of symbolically.

The second and third chapters of the book contain John's individual letters to the seven churches, put forth as the words of the Risen Christ, whom we met in John's first amazing vision. Each letter evaluates how that particular church is doing, and then offers either threats or encouragement. The seven churches are facing tests — being persecuted and in some cases being seduced by the attractions of the surrounding culture. If they are facing these tests properly, The Risen Christ, through John, gives them a pat on the back. If they are failing, he lets them have it.

For example, he writes to the church in Philadelphia: "I know your works. You have kept my word and not denied my name. I will keep you from the hour of trial that is coming on the whole world to test the inhabitants of the earth. I will write on you the name of my God."

He's not quite so happy with some of the other churches. To the church at Laodicea he writes, "I know your works. You are neither hot nor cold. I will spit you out of my mouth."

And to the church at Sardis he writes, "I know your works; you have a name of being alive, but you are dead. I have not found your works perfect in the sight of my God."

In both of those cases, the letters offer the churches one last chance to get their acts together before the coming end of the world.

Chapters 4 through 22 contain the series of visions that fill the rest of the book. This series begins with John seeing an open door and peeking through to another layer of reality. Nobody has ever summarized these 19 chapters of material as well as Marcus Borg, so I won't try to improve on it. This is Borg's overview of what John sees when he peeks through the door:

> The section begins with a vision of God enthroned in heaven, surrounded by 24 elders clothed in white crowns with gold on their heads. Four beasts are around the throne, each with six wings and eyes in the wings — strange creatures from another world. From the throne itself come lightning and thunder and voices.
>
> It continues with a vision of the lamb that was slain but that now lives and is worthy to open the seven seals of the scroll of judgment. As the seven seals are opened, we see the four horsemen of the apocalypse riding forth upon the earth, bringing war, famine, pestilence, and death. Then there is a great earthquake, the sky blackens, the stars fall from the heavens, and the sky rolls up like a scroll. The seventh seal is opened, and it introduces another series of seven judgments: seven angels begin to blow seven trumpets in succession. The blowing of the trumpets unleashes another series of plagues and catastrophes on the earth, including giant locusts that look like horses equipped for battle (bearing tails

like scorpions and making noise like many chariots) and an immense army of two hundred million invading from the east.

At the start of chapter twelve, we see a vision of a woman clothed like the sun, a crown of twelve stars on her head and the moon under her feet. She is giving birth to a child whom a great red dragon immediately tries to devour. At the same time, war breaks out in heaven: the archangel Michael and his angles battle against the great dragon, who loses and is cast down to earth.

In chapter thirteen, a beast with seven heads and ten horns to whom the dragon has given authority rises out of the sea and takes control of the earth. The number of the beast, we are told, is 666. Then seven angels pour out upon the earth the seven bowls of the wrath of God, and we are shown the judgment and destruction of the "great harlot" who rides upon the beast and whose name is "Babylon the Great." This is soon followed by the second coming of Christ on a white horse. Christ leads the army clad in white robes against the armies of the beast and destroys them, their bodies becoming food for carrion birds that gorge themselves with their flesh. The dragon, now named "the devil" and "Satan," is cast into a bottomless pit for a thousand years, during which Christ and the saints rule. After a thousand years, Satan is released, and with Gog and Magog he fights a final battle and is again defeated. Then the last judgment occurs: all the dead, great and small, are raised, the book of life is opened, and all whose names are not in it are cast into the lake of fire, along with the devil, the beast, death, and Hades.

After all of this, at the beginning of chapter 21,

> comes the magnificent concluding vision. The New Jerusalem, adorned as a bride for her new husband, descends from the sky — a city in which there will be no more tears, no pain, no death. The city has no need of a temple, for its temple is the Lord God The Almighty and the Lamb. Nor does the city have need of sun or moon, for the glory of God will be its light, and its lamp the Lamb of God. Through it flows the river of the water of life, and in it grows the tree of life whose leaves are for the healing of the nations. There, the seven servants of God will worship God and the Lamb. I quote Revelation: "They will see God's face, and God's name will be on their foreheads. And there will be no more night; they need no light of lamp or sun, for the Lord God will be their light, and they will reign forever and ever.

That concludes Borg's summary of revelation, and it is some story! It's easy to understand why some people have wondered if there were some psychedelic mushrooms growing on the island of Patmos. The question, of course, is whether we believe that all the things John writes about in Revelation are destined to happen at some time in the future, or whether a scholarly examination of the story can provide us with another explanation of those mysterious symbols and amazing images we find in the pages of that book.

The most popular way of reading the Revelation of John is to use a futurist interpretation, to insist it is all true and soon to happen. After all, it's in the Bible. Through the years, people have taken a fundamentalist view of the inerrancy of the Bible, combined that with a literal reading of the fanciful imagery of apocalyptic literature and managed to scare people witless over the book of Revelation.

But there is another way of reading this book. All those images, all those amazing visions are meant to symbolize people and things found in the ancient world, the world in which John wrote the story. Perhaps we should take seriously the words of Raymond Brown, one of the great New Testament scholars of the 20th century: "God has not revealed to human beings details about how the world began or how the world will end, and failing to recognize that, one is likely to misread both the first book and the last book of the Bible. The author of Revelation did not know how or when the world will end, and neither does anybody else."

9

Marcus Borg's Analysis of The Revelation of John

We now examine the two ways of reading the Revelation of John. One may read it as a futuristic vision of things soon to happen, and another may view it as a symbolic story about the first-century world in which the author lived. I am again indebted to Marcus Borg's *Reading the Bible Again for the First Time* for much of the information in this chapter.

According to a 1980 Gallup Poll, two-thirds of Americans — not only Christians, mind you, but two-thirds of all Americans — have "no doubts" that Jesus will come again. Another poll conducted in 2002 finds that 59 percent of Americans believe that the events depicted in the book of Revelation will actually occur. Make no mistake about it, the book of Revelation has been frightening people since it was included in the Christian Bible around 400 C.E. Over the centuries, people have viewed Revelation as a sort of scary and mysterious addendum to the Bible. But it wasn't until the 20th century that a literal reading of that book became the theological foundation for a segment of the church.

For this, we can thank a man named Cyrus Scofield, who published the Scofield Reference Bible in 1909. This abomination still adorns the bookshelf of every fire-and-brimstone, here-comes-the-end-of-the-world preacher in America. Scofield's theory holds that God divided world history into seven ages, or dispensations, and that the final age, when Christ physically comes again to rule on earth, is about to happen, precisely as described in Revelation.

Scofield poured over the Bible, and in effect turned it into a book of clues and riddles. According to him, all of scripture is a puzzle to be deciphered, with mysterious and secret meanings everywhere — and those clues give us a chance of escaping the coming wrath of God. Fortunately for all of humanity, Cyrus Scofield appeared in the nick of time. His reference Bible is the key which unlocked the truth hidden from past generations.

Scofield set the stage, and as we can see by the amazing success of the *Left Behind* book series by Tim LaHaye and Jerry B. Jenkins, there has been no shortage of people willing to cash in on people's fears. The end of the world is big business.

The futurist interpretation of Revelation is that the book accurately describes things that are soon to happen in this world. Three premises are foundational to this interpretation. One, the Bible is literally true. Second, what Revelation describes has not yet happened. And third, therefore, all the things described in Revelation must still be going to happen in the future.

Accepting these ideas turns Revelation into a puzzle filled with clues and symbols about the signs that will precede the Second Coming of Christ and the end of the world. This end-of-the-world theorizing about the book of Revelation reached its zenith in the 1970s when Hal Lindsey wrote the book *The Late Great Planet Earth*. Since that book was so popular (it was the best selling non-fiction book in the decade of the 70s), we'll use his theories to illustrate a futurist interpretation of Revelation.

Lindsey argues that the signs of the end-times are all around us, and the biggest sign of all is the establishment of the state of Israel in 1948. There are biblical passages that indicate the people of Israel will once again live in their own land, as a nation, when the time for the end of the world arrives. That situation has existed since 1948. So the stage has been set.

Lindsey then goes through and systematically decodes the language of Revelation and applies it to the world today. For example, consider these words of Revelation from chapter six:

> When he opened the sixth seal, I looked, and there came a great earthquake; the sun became black as sackcloth, the full moon became like blood, and the stars of the sky fell to the earth.... The sky vanished like a scroll rolling itself up, and every mountain and island was removed from its place.

That passage, says Lindsey, describes a thermonuclear exchange. The "stars of the sky falling to earth" are orbiting nuclear bombs reentering the atmosphere. The sky "rolling up like a scroll" is a description of what happens to the atmosphere when a nuclear bomb is detonated.

Consider these words from the ninth chapter of Revelation:

> Then the sixth angel blew his trumpet, and I heard a voice saying, "Release the four angels who are bound at the great river Euphrates." So the four angels were released, who had been held ready for the hour, the day, the month and the year to kill a third of humankind. The number of the troops of cavalry was two hundred million.

Hal Lindsey figures that passage must surely be referring to Communist China. Who else has a population large enough to field an army of two hundred million?

Here's one more quote from Revelation, again from chapter nine. Guess how Lindsey interprets this passage:

> Locusts appeared like horses equipped for battle. On their heads were what looked like crowns of gold; their faces were like human faces, their hair like women's hair, and their teeth like lion's teeth; they had scales like iron breastplates, and the noise of their wings was like the noise of many chariots with horses rushing into battle. They have tails like scorpions, with stingers, and in their tails is the power to harm people for five months.

Lindsey concludes that John of Patmos was given a vision of an attack helicopter. He doesn't bother to explain where on modern attack helicopters one places "crowns of gold" and "human faces," let alone "women's hair."

Lindsey recognizes the importance of the 10-horned beast from the sea in Revelation 13, and he understands that it has something to do with Rome. He concludes that it refers to an updated Roman Empire consisting of a 10-nation confederacy. To Lindsey, it is obvious that this is the group known as the European Economic Community, a group consisting of 10 member nations, formed by the Treaty of Rome during the 1970s.

Therefore, the time is near for the rapture, the final tribulation, the battle of Armageddon, the Second Coming of Christ and the last judgment. In the rapture, true Christians will be spared the great suffering that will arrive with the end-times, because they will be taken up from the earth to meet Jesus in heaven. According to Revelation, that suffering, known as the tribulation, begins with the opening of the seven seals, the blowing of the seven trumpets, the pouring out of the seven bowls, all of which unleashes God's awful wrath upon the world. The tribulation ends with the battle of Armageddon and the defeat of the beast's armies by the returning warrior from heaven, Jesus Christ.

To read Revelation in this manner, with a futurist interpretation, affects the heart of the Christian message. The gospel, or the good news, becomes the message that you can be saved from the awful wrath of our angry God by believing the right things about Jesus. The focus of the Christian faith becomes saving yourself and those you love from the horrendous, ugly fate that God has planned for most of humanity. Consider the implications for everyday life. Why worry about things like the environment and social justice if the world is about to end? Forget the world! Get saved, hunker down, wait.

We can't deny that Hal Lindsey's fantasizing about Revelation has attracted millions of followers. And the idea that Revelation is in some way foretelling future events is accepted by a wide range of Christians, including many who reject Lindsey's interpretation. They don't think the Revelation of John can be precisely decoded as in *The Late Great Planet Earth*, but they do believe it speaks in vague and mysterious ways about the coming end of the world.

The question, of course, is what alternative do we have to approaching the book as an actual foretelling of the end of the world? Whether that cataclysmic ending is coming next week or a million years in the future, must we believe that Revelation, in some way, tells of things that are destined to literally happen at some point?

We have another way of approaching the Revelation of John, namely, to interpret it as a reflection of the past, a symbolic history of the world in which the author lived 2,000 years ago. The first thing we have to do when approaching the book from this perspective is to take seriously the fact that Revelation was a letter, and the letter was not written to 21st-century Americans. It was written to seven specific churches in Asia. This takes no leap of faith. John of Patmos says at the beginning of the book, "I'm writing this letter to the seven churches in Asia" and then proceeds to name those seven churches.

And while there is no doubt that John is talking about the

future, he is most certainly talking about the near future. He describes the things he envisions as "what must soon take place" and says his words must be read aloud to the churches as soon as possible because "the time is near." He concludes his letter by mentioning five times that the end is imminent.

While it may be true, as some argue, that a thousand years are like a single day to God, it seems clear that the author of this book was writing about his own world's immediate future. Let's look at a few passages within the body of the letter that reveal John was addressing the issues of his own time.

In chapter 13, the 10-horned beast from the sea rules the world and demands worship. The Roman emperors ruled John's world. Those emperors had temples throughout the empire in which they were hailed as lord and god. As we discovered in chapter 8, the much ballyhooed number 666, the number of the beast, the sign of the antichrist, has kept prophets of doom on the lookout for the one who will rise to do battle against the forces of good. In John's world, the forces fighting against good, those forces persecuting the church, were the powers under the control of the Roman emperor. And using an ancient coding technique known as gematria, the number 666 translates as "Caesar Nero."

Consider John's vision of the "great whore" in chapter 17, another symbolic reference to the Roman Empire. This woman, dressed in "royal" attire, rides upon the beast, and her name is "Babylon the Great." Interpretation can be confusing, because the Babylonian empire vanished 600 years before John wrote this letter, but here is a key point.

The religious world of the Jews, from which Christianity sprang and upon which Christianity is built, was centered on the temple. Solomon built the first temple in the 10th century B.C.E, and in 586 B.C.E. Babylon destroyed the temple. This was the beginning of the Babylonian captivity, the greatest tragedy the Jewish people had faced up to that point. After the Babylonian captivity ended, the temple was rebuilt, and it again stood as the holiest place on earth until 70 C.E. In that year, just a few decades before John wrote this letter, a foreign army once again rode into Jerusalem and leveled the temple. And to this day, the temple has never been rebuilt. Who destroyed the temple for good, surely one of the pivotal moments in the life of the first-century faithful? Answer: Rome. The name "Babylon" was synonymous with "evil empire." And in first-century Christian and Jewish circles, Babylon had become the symbolic name for Rome.

Some may think this is stretching the point a bit, claiming that John is referring to Rome when he uses the word *Babylon*. This is a critical point, because if *Rome* and *Babylon* are synonymous to John, then all of John's imagery is aimed not at the rising evil powers of the modern world, but solely at the Roman empire of his day. Consider this: The great whore whose name is Babylon the Great is seated on seven mountains. Throughout history, Rome has been known as the city built on seven hills. And then John does something he rarely does in this letter: He actually interprets the symbol for us. This is a quote from Revelation: "The woman you saw is the great city that rules over the kings of the earth."

When you take into consideration that the seven churches to which he addressed his letter would have found no meaning in predictions about the European Economic Community and attack helicopters, it becomes evident that John was writing about his own time. Further, there can be little doubt about the identity of the great enemy of God he rails against throughout the book. That enemy is Rome.

Remember: Christians were being fed to lions in Rome as a way of entertaining the masses. And there were occasions when Christians were tied to crosses along the road leading away from the Coliseum and then burned alive to provide lighting for those who were leaving the evening's entertainment. These things were real. They happened. John and those first-century churches didn't need to look thousands of years into the future to find the antichrist.

John used the literary genre of apocalyptic literature, which was popular at that time, to both warn and encourage the churches in his region. He certainly was writing about the future, predicting God's revenge against Rome. But he was writing about the immediate future of his world, not the immediate future of ours.

There is an underlying message in the Revelation of John that exists as the real purpose of the letter. Marcus Borg, to whom I am indebted for the content of these chapters on Revelation, summarizes John's message as threefold:

First, even though it doesn't seem that way, Christ is Lord; Caesar and the beast, the powers of evil, are not.

Second, God will soon act to overthrow the rule of the beast and its incarnation in Caesar.

And third, the churches should therefore have faith and persevere through the present evil.

With that, I bring these reflections on Revelation to a close.

I confess I tend to be one of those people who, like Martin Luther, wish somebody had thrown the Revelation of John into some river long ago. As long as there are people intent on scaring others into the Christian faith and cashing in on their fears, the book of Revelation's influence in the Christian faith will continue to be problematic.

But if we accept it for what it is, we have to admit Revelation holds a powerful place in the Bible, largely because of the way it completes the symbolic story we find in Genesis, the first chapter of the Bible. The Bible begins with God's creation of the world and humanity's alienation from God. The Bible ends with the reunion of God and humanity, with the overcoming of the exile from the Garden of Eden. Finally, God truly rules. Every tear shall be wiped away, and the river of life flows through humankind's new home, God's new and perfect creation. And there, we will all see God and joyfully worship together forevermore.

Despite all the problems we have with the book of Revelation, it is hard to imagine a more powerful ending to the Bible.

10

The New...Old Fundamentals

I was in the midst of delivering the sermons that served as the basis for this book when a young woman visited our church for the first time. She said she appreciated the fact that I was not attacking fundamentalists, that I was simply questioning whether it was neccessary for a person to believe in the fundamentals in order to be a Christian. And then she asked, "But what do you believe?"

That's a fair question. I have accused some of my favorite theologians of being more capable of dismantling the faith than they are at putting it back together. And this really strikes home for those of us who are comfortable in a Congregational Church, where freedom of thought is so important. Evangelicals, who often go door to door spreading the gospel, joke that a Congregationalist is a person who puts on his best suit, rings your doorbell and then just stands there with nothing to say.

I will now attempt to define what we believe, what it is that makes us call ourselves Christians. In doing so, many will accuse me of re-writing the faith. They will say I am turning away from true Christianity and inventing a new faith. But they could not be more wrong.

In the first chapters of this work, we saw that fundamentalism is really a 19th- and 20th-century phenomenon. It is a reaction to the modern world. It is not so much a return to the roots of the

Christian faith as it is an insistence on thinking about Christianity with an ancient worldview, a return to the days when the earth stood still at the center of the universe, God was up in the sky and nobody had to deal with pesky issues such as evolution or the size and age of the universe.

Many of us have a real problem with pitting our religion against scientific truth. We look back in history and realize the church made a tragic mistake when it refused to accept the truth God has placed all around us. The church fought with all its might the idea that the earth is not the center of the universe. But no matter how deeply people of faith stuck their heads in the sand, nothing they could do would make the earth the center of the universe. That's not the way God made things.

So what happened when we faced the truth? Did God disappear? No! But our concept of God had to grow. God must be a whole lot bigger and whole lot more powerful than we previously imagined. God refused to remain in the little box we created for him.

When the fundamentalists today insist the universe is only 6,000 years old, an age they deduce by adding up the ages of biblical figures, they repeat the mistake the church made with regard to the earth's place in the universe. Likewise when they refuse to accept evolution as a valid scientific theory. But let's think of it this way. Which would be the greater God — the God who reigns over creation for 6,000 years or the God who reigns over creation for 14 billion years? And which God would inspire the most awe — the God who in an instant brought humanity into existence or the God who took billions of years of love and care to bring forth these amazing, questioning, God-seeking beings we call humans?

We should never pit God against the truth. God is always waiting for us squarely in the middle of any truth we find. And God is always greater and bigger and more awesome than anything we can imagine.

What are we to believe in such a magnificent creation? What is our anchor, our foundation, when our lives take place on a tiny speck of dust hurtling through space in an unimaginably vast universe? Does it matter whether a Christian believes Jesus was simply a great moral teacher or insists he was the incarnation of God? Shouldn't we all turn to Jesus for our answer?

Some say that's what fundamentalism does. True, fundamentalism is all about Jesus, but only in one narrow respect. Fundamentalists get caught up in believing what people have said about the nature of Jesus, believing in the virgin birth and the physical resurrection and the Second Coming in literal terms. But when I say we should turn to Jesus, I mean we should turn to Jesus of Nazareth, who walked this earth 2,000 years ago. I mean we should seriously consider what he actually had to say about life and religion and God.

This will offend more than fundamentalists. One very good theology professor I studied under in seminary was deeply insulted by those shirts and wristbands that say WWJD — "What Would Jesus Do?" He claimed that that saying missed the whole point. It's not important what Jesus would do, or even what he taught. What matters is who Jesus was — the holy Son of God who died for the sins of humanity. My argument was that even for those of us who believe Jesus was the true Son of God, we should still face life's difficult moments by asking ourselves *What would Jesus do?*

And so, knowing that our interpretation of the faith will not be acceptable to many, let's consider some new fundamentals on which to anchor our faith. And to do that, I suggest we go back to the old fundamentals. Not the fundamentals taught to us by modern fundamentalists. Not even to the teachings of 2,000 years of theologians and religious leaders of various stripes. But rather we should return to the fundamentals as taught by Jesus himself.

Our first fundamental is found in the three synoptic gospels.

We'll use the phrasing from the Gospel of Matthew. In this passage, Jesus tells us quite specifically what the first fundamental should be. There are more than 600 laws in the Torah — the first five books of the Bible. A Pharisee asks Jesus which commandment is the most important. Matthew 22:37-38 provides the answer: "Jesus said to him, 'You shall love the Lord your God with all your heart, and with all your soul, and with all your mind. This is the greatest and first commandment.' "

Surely that is the first fundamental of the Christian faith. We may understand the mystery of God in different ways, anything from a personal and benevolent Creator who is actively involved in our lives, to the more distant God of the Enlightenment thinkers and the founding fathers of this country. But we acknowledge that we do not call ourselves into being. We acknowledge that we do not bestow life upon ourselves. Life is a gift. And to that mystery from which our lives spring forth, we are lovingly surrendered, heart, soul and mind.

Loving God with heart, soul and mind: That is the heart of our faith. And we should consider the third element of our love of God — loving God with all our *minds*. This precludes us from sticking our heads in the sand. It is permissable to think about God. In fact, according to Jesus, involving our minds in our faith is foundational. Pretending the earth is flat and stationary at the center of the universe does not make it so. Pretending that the universe is only 6,000 years old does not make it so. We should embrace the mystery of creation, the amazing and complex truths we find all around us, always remembering that God is the creator of all truth. So our first fundamental is plain: Love God with your heart, soul and mind.

What is our second fundamental? Again, this is an easy one, because Jesus gives us the answer quite specifically. After revealing the greatest and first commandment, Jesus says, "And a second is like it: You shall love your neighbor as yourself. On those two commandments hang all the law and the prophets."

Let's think about that! On the two commandments — love of God and love of neighbor — hang all the law and the prophets. Jesus tells us with great specificity what religion is all about. He keeps it simple by telling us that anything beyond those two essential elements is a footnote to the faith.

Regarding love of neighbor as self, we should note that Jesus is telling us we should love ourselves. He doesn't say to love your neighbor and not care about what happens to you. He is saying that we should embrace the gift of life, that we should love our lives but not to the exclusion or detriment of others. Love life. Love people. So we have our foundation for the Christian faith, given to us by Jesus himself.

Fundamental number one:

Love God with your heart, soul and mind.

Fundamental number two:

Love your neighbor as yourself.

We could stop there. A person who attempts to love God and neighbor qualifies as a Christian. All the other elements of our faith are ornamental, decorations hung on those core values. That does not mean those decorations are bad or of no value. In fact, still relying on the words of Jesus, there are some other fundamentals that I have personally adopted as a part of my Christian faith.

The third fundamental for many of us is faith. Faith is derived from those first two fundamentals. We have faith that there really is a God who hears our prayers. We have faith that life acquires its full meaning when we truly love our neighbors as we love ourselves. But there is one more thing about faith that is foundational, perhaps the very core of what faith is really all about. To have real faith is to believe that this universe is a good thing. To have real faith is to believe that this amazing, confusing, beautiful, terrible world in which we find ourselves is good.

Too many people treat life in this world as some sort of test.

What matters most to them is the heaven that awaits us upon leaving this world. While it is perfectly valid to believe in something beyond the grave, to acknowledge that there is more to our being than these bodies of dust, it is also acceptable to view life in this world as a wonderful gift. It took God a long long time to call creatures forth from the dust, creatures capable of looking at the world around them and conceiving of God, asking questions about creation and worshipping the creator of it all. God surely did not go to such lengths so we could view our time on earth as something to be escaped.

There is a lot of pain in this world. It is easy for our thinking to stray into one of two extremes: That life is a meaningless accident, a fluke chemical reaction with no direction or purpose; or that life is simply a stopping-off point, a way of earning our way into a future heaven.

But faith, real faith, is life affirming. God is in control of what happens beyond the grave. We are given freedom to have a great deal of control over what happens on this side of the grave. Our faith tells us that this life is beautiful and worthwhile, a gift beyond all treasures.

Our fourth fundamental is joy, which grows out of the third fundamental. Shame on those who would turn the Christian faith into something dour and threatening! Joy is the mark of a faith-filled Christian. Why? Because the love a Christian feels for God and neighbor and the faith a Christian has in the goodness of the universe creates joy. Remember the words of Jesus from the 10th chapter of the Gospel of John: "I came that they may have life, and have it abundantly."

Abundant life. What an amazing concept. An abundant life would be a life that is lacking for nothing, a life filled with love, and peace, and enough material goods to make a person feel secure and unafraid. An abundant life would be a life filled with joy. And that, according to the words of Jesus, is why he lived on this earth in the first place.

The fifth and final fundamental of our faith is the only negative one. Looking at the Ten Commandments, we see a list of positives and negatives, do's and don'ts. Do worship God alone; don't make false idols. Do honor your mother and father; don't steal. We must include one fundamental in our list that includes a "don't," because this particular fundamental is so foundational in the ministry and teachings of Jesus: *Don't judge.*

Don't judge. We'll again turn to the Gospel of Matthew, Jesus' words from the Sermon on the Mount: "Do not judge, so that you may not be judged." The fact is, all fall short of the glory of God. In the light of God's perfection we each look like very sinful creatures. It is not our place to judge others. It is not our purpose in life to tell others how they must live, or think, or worship.

My main argument against fundamentalism is the way in which that approach to Christianity judges others. I recognize that I am guilty of making a judgment when I say this. Still, the ultimate judgment one could make against other human beings is to tell them they are going to hell, that they in no way stand in the grace of God. And that is what fundamentalism does. It claims that one is either a believer in the fundamentals and therefore saved, or one is judged to be lost and bound for hell. That, truly, is the ultimate judgment one person can make against another.

What we have here are two very different approaches to the Christian faith. The fundamentalist approach divides the world into the saved and the hell-bound, claiming that belief in seven specific fundamentals is the key to being saved. Let's recap those seven fundamentals. First, the Bible is incapable of error. Second, Jesus is fully God. Third, Jesus was born of a virgin. Fourth, Jesus performed miracles that defy the laws of nature. Fifth, substitutionary atonement — the sacrifice of Jesus — is the means by which people are saved. Sixth, Jesus Christ was physically resurrected from the grave and physically ascended into heaven. And seventh, Jesus will return again in physical form to judge the living and the dead.

The approach I am suggesting is a return to the actual teachings of Jesus, refusing to draw a line in the sand between the "saved" and the "unsaved." I propose five "new" old fundamentals. The first two are primary. First, Christians love God with heart, soul and mind. Second, Christians try to live life so that they love neighbor as self. Third, Christians have faith in the goodness of God's creation and the goodness of life. Fourth, Christians live lives filled with joy, because that is the mark of one who loves God, loves neighbor and has faith in the goodness of life. And fifth, Christians do not judge other people.

I believe these are true fundamentals of our faith. It is important to note that one can believe in these five new (actually old) fundamentals, and still believe in most of the fundamentals promoted by modern fundamentalism. Consider ideas like the virgin birth and the physical resurrection. We should be careful about dismissing such things too quickly. A person in the first century would not have believed he lived on a round planet, rotating as it hurtles through space, revolving around the sun, which is actually a star, in a universe with billions more stars than one could possibly count. A first-century human being would have sworn by the indisputable fact that we are standing on a flat and stationary earth, and the sun, moon and stars are in motion around us.

The more we learn, the more incomprehensible the universe gets. And science, rather than explaining everything about creation, instead leads us to more and more questions. We should all be very cautious about drawing lines in the sand when pondering what is and is not possible. Every time we think we have things figured out, God surprises us.

Turning to quantum physics with its multidimensional universe, we realize that we really are children, just beginning to see the wonder of the world. It is more amazing, more complex, more majestic than we realized. And that means God is more amazing, more complex and more majestic than we realized. With our understanding of creation still evolving, can we really know what God is and is not capable of doing?

And so we open ourselves to the mystery and anchor ourselves on our foundational fundamentals. We may differ over how Jesus came into this world and how he left it. But we love God and neighbor, we take joy in life and have faith that this amazing creation is all worthwhile, and we refuse to judge other people as they embrace the mystery of life.

There is a word for people who respond to life in such a manner. They are called *Christians*.

Annotated Bibliography

Karen Armstrong

The Battle for God

Karen Armstrong's thorough and thoughtful analysis focuses on the rise of fundamentalism in the three monotheistic religions. She examines Protestant fundamentalism in the United States, Jewish fundamentalism in Israel and Islamic fundamentalism in Egypt and Iran. Armstrong maintains that a new type of civilization arose in the West in the 16th century, and new forms of faith developed in response to this new world. By the 20th century, some form of fundamentalism had developed in every major faith tradition. Armstrong reveals how and why those groups emerged, the dangers involved and ways to defuse the growing tension that exists between fundamentalists of different faiths.

Bruce Bawer

Stealing Jesus

The subtitle of this book is *How Fundamentalism Betrays Christianity*. Bawer views Christian fundamentalism as a harmful and dangerous cancer on the church. His passion for the subject makes *Stealing Jesus* an enjoyable and worthwhile read, although it should be noted that he is caustically strident in his attack on fundamentalism. He holds no punches as he takes on the leading figures of the religious right.

Marcus Borg
The God We Never Knew

Borg begins this book by reminding the reader that he is a Jesus scholar and not a theologian. What follows, however, is a beautifully crafted and very readable book of theology. Borg revisits the God so many of us discovered in our younger years, a God who is to be feared. He then explains why he has accepted panentheism as the best way of conceiving of God. From the relationship between God and Jesus to what happens when we die, this book covers a lot of ground in remarkably plain English.

Marcus Borg
The Heart of Christianity

This book is Marcus Borg's most comprehensive overview of the Christian faith. He begins by asking what it means to be a Christian in the modern world, and then attempts to get to the "heart" of the matter. In Part One he examines the Christian tradition, saying faith is "the way of the heart," the Bible is "the heart of the tradition," God is "the heart of reality" and Jesus is "the heart of God."

In Part Two, Borg turns to the Christian life, discussing such matters as the Kingdom of God, sin, salvation and being "born again." This is the best book I have found on the subject of modern Christianity.

Marcus Borg
Meeting Jesus Again for the First Time

This is the book that put Marcus Borg on the map, and deservedly so. At the heart of this work lies Borg's contention that when we talk about Jesus we should separate the historical Jesus from the Christ of faith. Borg calls these two ways of thinking about Jesus the "pre-Easter Jesus" and the "post-Easter Jesus." Borg contends that the pre-Easter Jesus was a thoroughly Jewish teacher of wisdom for whom God was an experiential reality. The post-Easter Jesus is the Christ upon which the church has been built.

Marcus Borg
Reading the Bible Again for the First Time

Chapter 10 of this book by Borg served as the foundation for chapters 8 and 9 of *Think Again*. *Reading the Bible Again for the First Time* shows great respect for scripture without worshipping the Bible. Borg explains how to read the Bible for spiritual insight without falling into the trap of making religion an exercise in superstition.

Marcus Borg and N.T. Wright
The Meaning of Jesus: Two Visions

This is an essential read for anybody wanting to take the Christian faith seriously. Both Borg and Wright are excellent scholars. Borg is a leading liberal thinker, and N.T. Wright is a thoughtful orthodox thinker. *The Meaning of Jesus* is a dialogue between these two scholars. Subjects include the birth of Jesus, the teachings of Jesus, the divinity of Jesus, the death of Jesus, the resurrection and the second coming. Wright and Borg have radically different views of the Christian faith, and each represents his particular view intelligently and courteously.

Robert Farrar Capon
Kingdom, Grace, Judgment

This excellent book is subtitled *Paradox, Outrage, and Vindication in the Parables of Jesus*. Capon divides the parables into three categories: parables of the kingdom, parables of grace and parables of judgment. The power of this book lies in the fact that

Capon believes the saving power of Christ applies to all people, not just some elect minority. Seeing the parables of Jesus interpreted with this universalist understanding is enlightening and refreshing.

John Dominic Crossan
Jesus: a Revolutionary Biography

Crossan is one of the premier Jesus scholars in the world today. The Jesus we find in his many books is a very human teacher with a politically powerful message that literally changed the world.

Bart D. Ehrman
Lost Christianities

Ehrman takes the reader on a journey through the first centuries of the church. We discover that there were many forms of Christianity in those years, most having been suppressed or forgotten. One particular strain of the faith prevailed, and all other forms of Christianity were labeled as heresies. *Lost Christianities* is the story of the power and politics that led to modern "orthodox" Christianity.

Matthew Fox
The Coming of the Cosmic Christ

Matthew Fox is a prolific and controversial author. In *The Coming of the Cosmic Christ* he proposes a radically different way of viewing Christian theology. He compares the crucifixion of Christ to the dying of Mother Earth and the loss of wisdom and creativity. He draws an analogy between the resurrection of Jesus and the rebirth of mysticism in the modern world. And importantly, with regard to *Think Again*, Fox provides a vision of the second coming of Christ as the healing of our planet and a global renaissance of compassion and creativity.

Bede Griffiths
Return to the Center

I include this book in the bibliography not because of any direct correlation to *Think Again*, but rather because it is the most spiritually powerful book in my library. Griffiths was an English monk who lived in an ashram in India for 35 years. Deeply influenced by the surrounding Hindu culture, Griffiths integrates Eastern and Western religious thinking almost seamlessly.

There is scarcely a page in this entire book that does not draw me out of the world of my senses, connecting me with the center of centers, the very Spirit of God who calls all of creation into being.

Philip Gulley and James Mulholland
If God Is Love

Gulley and Mulholland were each raised in a fear-based version of the Christian faith, with religion based on threats, requirements, rewards and punishment. Their faith journeys led them to become universalists. The recurring theme is that God's love is the most powerful thing in the universe, and ultimately love conquers all. The authors insist that how we live is at least as important as what we believe. Putting away our judgment is the surest way to open ourselves to God.

Carter Heyward
Saving Jesus from Those Who Are Right

Heyward is a progressive feminist theologian. Rather than focus on the person of Jesus as an exalted being, she presents Jesus as our brother. There is sacred power in our attempts to embody the right relations Jesus stood for. Like most feminist theologians, Heyward's Christology is incarnational (bottom up) as opposed to top down. She insists we anchor our faith not on theological conjecturing about the nature of the Risen Christ, but rather with the person of Jesus who remains our intimate teacher.

Peter C. Hodgson and Robert H. King
Christian Theology

This is the best theology textbook I have found. It is not an easy read but is well worth the effort. Hodgson and King edit the writings of some of the most prominent theological voices in the modern church. Virtually every theological subject is examined, from scripture, God, revelation and creation, to the church, Christ and salvation, the sacraments and Christian views toward other religions.

With each subject the book examines current thinking, the doctrine in its classical formulation, the evolution of thinking on the subject through church history, the challenges to the doctrine in the modern world, and issues for the future. This book is a classic, used in seminaries all over the world.

Charles Kimball
When Religion Becomes Evil

Kimball's specialty is comparative religion. In *When Religion Becomes Evil* he reveals how all religious traditions are susceptible to certain corruptions that turn religion into a negative force. He points out five warning signs that a religion is becoming corrupt: (1) absolute truth claims; (2) blind obedience; (3) establishing the "ideal" time; (4) the end justifies the means; and (5) declaring holy war.

Alister E. McGrath
Christian Theology: An Introduction

McGrath's book is a widely used seminary textbook. It is both detailed and comprehensive. If I were to recommend just one theology textbook, this would be my choice.

William C. Placher
Narratives of a Vulnerable God

William Placher is not a progressive thinker with regard to Christianity. In fact, he is very orthodox. But his keen intellect makes him an important voice in the modern church. I include *Narratives of a Vulnerable God* in this bibliography because of the impact it had on my faith journey. The three parts of the book are titled "God," "Diversities" and "Discipleship."

In Part One (God) Placher writes about two of the most difficult ideas in Christianity: the concept of eternity and the concept of the Trinity. In both cases he impacted my entire worldview. It is not an easy read, but it is worth the effort.

John Polkinghorne
Belief in God in an Age of Science

John Polkinghorne is an internationally known theoretical physicist and a theologian. He insists that science and faith are not mutually exclusive fields of inquiry. I quote from the forward of Polkinghorne's *Belief in God in an Age of Science*: "The book presents a series of variations on a fundamental theme: if reality is generously and adequately construed, then knowledge will be seen to be one; if rationality is generously and adequately construed, then science and theology will be seen as partners in a common quest for understanding."

F. Schleiermacher
On Religion: Speeches to Its Cultured Despisers

Friedrick Schleiermacher is widely regarded as the father of liberal theology. This book was written in 1799, at a time when many enlightened thinkers had relegated religion to the realm of superstition. Schleiermacher fully embraced the scientific discoveries of the Enlightenment, while insisting that religion is the most important aspect of an authentic human life.

Schleiermacher rejected ideas such as the virgin birth, physical resurrection and other miracles, insisting that authentic religion is based on a feeling of absolute dependence on God for our very existence. This book represents a paradigm shift in Christianity that continues to affect the church today.

John Shelby Spong
A New Christianity for a New World

Bishop Spong is perhaps the most controversial figure in the modern church. He has written books that question original sin, the virgin birth, the resurrection, and over the course of his career has taken issue with literally every sacred cow of the Christian faith. He has sometimes been accused of being more capable of dismantling the faith than of putting it back together. In *A New Christianity for a New World* he attempts to answer his critics by laying the foundation for what he believes.

John Shelby Spong
Why Christianity Must Change or Die

Probably Spong's most famous work, *Why Christianity Must Change or Die* is practically a handbook for progressive Christianity. He begins by taking on the historic creeds for their ancient worldview and moves to a theme that is recurrent throughout his works: Theism is not a working model for God.

Many theologians would argue with Spong's insistence that theism necessarily places God "up in the sky," but his message is clear. There is no external deity to which humanity can turn for answers. The divine is found in the concrete reality of everyday life.

Spong posits Jesus as a spirit person and places great emphasis on the teachings of Jesus of Nazareth as opposed to confessional statements about Jesus. Insisting that many aspects of our Christian heritage must be recognized as primitive and superstitious, Spong champions the God who is the Ground of Being, the universal presence from which all life springs.

Wayne Teasdale
The Mystic Heart

Wayne Teasdale is an interreligious monk and mystic who believes that the same mystical core lies at the root of all religions. A student of Bede Griffiths, Teasdale finds a mystical unity between Eastern and Western religion. According to Teasdale, each of us is a mystic at heart, and he points the reader toward the eight practical elements of our universal spirituality: solidarity with all life, moral capacity, non-violence, self-knowledge, selfless service, simplicity of lifestyle, daily practice and serving as a prophetic witness in the causes of justice, peace and protecting creation. *The Mystic Heart* is one of the most inspiring books I have ever read.

Ken Wilber
Quantum Questions

Ken Wilber is a brilliant thinker and the author of many books. His specialty is transpersonal psychology, and he is a leading proponent of what he calls an integral worldview, integrating science, faith and morality into a single system. *A Brief History of Everything* is a good place to get an overview of Wilber's philosophy. *In Quantum Questions*, Wilber edits the mystical writings of the world's great 20th-century physicists. They are all here: Heisenberg, Schroedinger, Einstein, De Broglie, Jeans, Planck, Pauli and Eddington. Each of these great scientific thinkers arrives at a point where he falls silent before the mystery of being itself. Contrary to what most consider a "scientific" worldview, these physicists conclude that matter is not the ultimate reality. Mind precedes matter, and all of reality is grounded in the mystery of Spirit.

This is a very good book for those who have turned away from religion because of the superstitious tendencies of many religious people, in the process rejecting all forms of religion and spirituality. It is both enlightening and humbling to see these great minds surrendered in silent awe before the mystery of God.

Bibliography

Armstrong, Karen. *The Battle for God.* New York: Alfred A. Knopf, 2000.

Bawer, Bruce. *Stealing Jesus: How Fundamentalism Betrays Christianity.* New York: Three Rivers Press, 1997.

Borg, Marcus. *The God We Never Knew: Beyond Dogmatic Religion to a More Authentic Contemporary Faith.* New York: HarperSanFrancisco, 1997.

_______. *The Heart of Christianity: Rediscovering a Life of Faith.* New York: HarperSanFrancisco, 2003

_______. *Meeting Jesus Again for the First Time: The Historical Jesus & The Heart of Contemporary Faith.* New York: HarperSanFrancisco, 1994.

_______. *Reading the Bible Again for the First Time: Taking the Bible Seriously but Not Literally.* New York: HarperSanFrancisco, 2001.

Borg, Marcus and N.T. Wright. *The Meaning of Jesus: Two Visions.* New York: HarperSanFrancisco, 1999.

Capon, Robert Farrar. *Kingdom, Grace, Judgment: Paradox, Outrage, and Vindication in the Parables of Jesus*. Cambridge, UK: Wm. B. Eerdmans, 2002.

Crossan, John Dominic. Jesus: *A Revolutionary Biography*. New York: HarperSanFrancisco, 1995.

Ehrman, Bart D. *Lost Christianities: The Battles for Scripture and the Faith We Never Knew*. New York: Oxford University Press, 2003.

Fox, Matthew. *The Coming of the Cosmic Christ*. New York: HarperSanFrancisco, 1988.

Griffiths, Bede. *Return to the Center*. Springfield, Illinois: Templegate Publishers, 1977.

Gulley, Philip and James Mulholland. *If God Is Love: Rediscovering Grace in an Ungracious World*. New York: HarperSanFrancisco, 2004.

Heyward, Carter. *Saving Jesus From Those Who Are Right: Rethinking What It Means to be Christian*. Minneapolis: Fortress Press, 1999.

Hodgson, Peter C. and Robert H. King. *Christian Theology: An Introduction to Its Traditions and Tasks*. Minneapolis: Fortress Press, 1994.

Kimball, Charles. *When Religion Becomes Evil*. New York: HarperSanFrancisco, 2002.

McGrath, Alister. *Christian Theology: An Introduction*. Oxford, UK: Blackwell Publishers, 1994.

Placher, William C. *Narratives of a Vulnerable God: Christ, Theology, and Scripture*. Louisville: Westminster John Knox Press, 1994.

Polkinghorne, John. *Belief in God in an Age of Science*. New Haven: Yale University Press, 1998.

Schleiermacher, Friedrich. *On Religion: Speeches to Its Cultured Despisers*. Louisville: Westminster John Knox Press, 1994.

Spong, John Shelby. *A New Christianity for a New World: Why Traditional Faith is Dying and How a New Faith is Being Born.* New York: HarperSanFrancisco, 2001.

_______. *Why Christianity Must Change or Die: A Bishop Speaks to Believers in Exile.* New York: HarperSanFrancisco, 1999.

Teasdale, Wayne. *The Mystic Heart: Discovering a Universal Spirituality in the World's Religions.* Novato, California: New World Library, 2001.

Wilber, Ken. *Quantum Questions: Mystical Writings of the World's Great Physicists.* Boston: Shambhala Publications, 1984.

Index